100 THINGS

EVERY DESIGNER NEEDS TO KNOW ABOUT PEOPLE

SUSAN WEINSCHENK, PH.D.

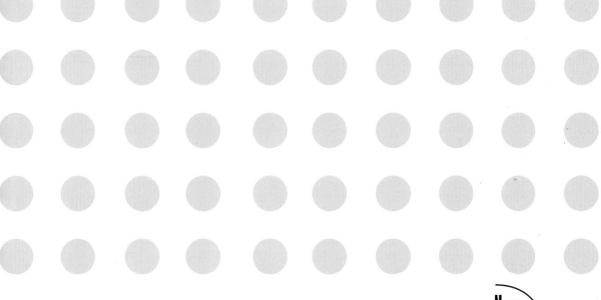

New
Riders

VOICES THAT MATTER™

100 Things Every Designer Needs to Know About People
Susan Weinschenk, Ph.D.

New Riders
1249 Eighth Street
Berkeley, CA 94710
510/524-2178
510/524-2221 (fax)

Find us on the Web at: www.newriders.com
To report errors, please send a note to errata@peachpit.com

New Riders is an imprint of Peachpit, a division of Pearson Education.

Project Editor: Michael J. Nolan
Development Editor: Jeff Riley
Production Editor: Tracey Croom
Copyeditor: Gretchen Dykstra
Indexer: Joy Dean Lee
Proofreader: Jan Seymour
Cover Designer: Mimi Heft
Interior Designer and Compositor: Maureen Forys, Happenstance Type-O-Rama

ISBN 13: 978-0-321-76753-0
ISBN 10: 0-321-76753-5

9 8 7

Printed and bound in the United States of America

ACKNOWLEDGEMENTS

Many thanks to my great editing team at Peachpit, especially the late night email exchanges with Jeff Riley my development editor. Thanks to Michael Nolan (acquisitions editor) for encouraging me in writing this one and sheparding it through the process. Thanks to Guthrie Weinschenk for his photos, Maisie Weinschenk for her great ideas, and Peter Weinschenk for his support and patience. And a thank you to all those who follow my blog, come to my presentations, and in general listen to me talk about psychology. You give me valuable ideas, opinions, and are the reason I keep searching out and writing about psychology and design.

DEDICATION

Dedicated to the memory of Miles and Jeanette Schwartz. Wish you were here to share the book with.

CONTENTS

HOW PEOPLE READ

HOW PEOPLE REMEMBER

HOW PEOPLE THINK

HOW PEOPLE FOCUS THEIR ATTENTION

WHAT MOTIVATES PEOPLE

PEOPLE ARE SOCIAL ANIMALS

HOW PEOPLE FEEL

PEOPLE MAKE MISTAKES

HOW PEOPLE DECIDE

THE PSYCHOLOGY OF DESIGN

Whether you're designing a Web site or a medical device—or something somewhere in between—your audience is comprised of the people who will benefit from that design.

And the totality of your audience's experience is profoundly impacted by what you know—or *don't know*—about them.

How do they think? How do they decide? What motivates them to click or purchase or whatever it is you want them to do?

You'll learn those things in this book.

You'll also learn what grabs their attention, what errors they will make and why, as well as other things that will help you design better.

And you'll design better because I've already done most of the heavy lifting for you. I'm one of those strange people who likes to read research. Lots and lots of research. So I read—or in some cases, *re-read*—dozens of books and hundreds of research articles. I picked my favorite theories, concepts, and research studies.

Then I combined them with experience I've gained throughout the many years I've been designing technology interfaces.

And you're holding the result: 100 things I think you need to know about people.

HOW
PEOPLE
SEE

Vision trumps all the senses. Half of the brain's resources are dedicated to seeing and interpreting what we see. What our eyes physically perceive is only one part of the story. The images coming in to our brains are changed and interpreted. It's really our brains that are "seeing."

1 WHAT YOU SEE ISN'T WHAT YOUR BRAIN GETS

You think that as you're walking around looking at the world, your eyes are sending information to your brain, which processes it and gives you a realistic experience of "what's out there." But the truth is that what your brain comes up with *isn't* exactly what your eyes are seeing. Your brain is constantly interpreting everything you see. Take a look at **Figure 1.1**, for example.

What do you see? At first you probably see a triangle with a black border in the background, and an upside-down, white triangle on top of it. Of course, that's not really what's there, is it? In reality there are merely lines and partial circles. Your brain creates the shape of an upside-down triangle out of empty space, because that's what it expects to see. This particular illusion is called a Kanizsa triangle, named for the Italian psychologist Gaetano Kanizsa, who developed it in 1955. Now look at **Figure 1.2**, which creates a similar illusion with a rectangle.

THE BRAIN CREATES SHORTCUTS

Your brain creates these shortcuts in order to quickly make sense out of the world around you. Your brain receives millions of sensory inputs every second (the estimate is 40 million) and it's trying to make sense of all of that input. It uses rules of thumb, based on past experience, to make guesses about what you see. Most of the time that works, but sometimes it causes errors.

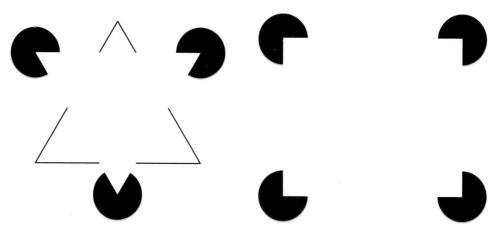

FIGURE 1.1 You see triangles, but they are not really there

FIGURE 1.2 An example of a Kanizsa rectangle

You can influence what people see, or think they see, by the use of shapes and colors. **Figure 1.3** shows how color can draw attention to one message over another.

FIGURE 1.3 Color and shapes can influence what people see

 If you need to see in the dark, don't look straight ahead.

The eye has 7 million cones that are sensitive to bright light and 125 million rods that are sensitive to low light. The cones are in the fovea (central area of vision) and rods are less central. So if you're in low light, you'll see better if you don't look right at the area you're trying to see.

 Optical illusions show us the errors

Optical illusions are examples of how the brain misinterprets what the eyes see. For example, in **Figure 1.4** the line on the left looks longer than the line on the right, but they're actually the same length. Named for Franz Müller-Lyer, who created it in 1889, this is one of the oldest optical illusions.

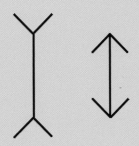

FIGURE 1.4 These lines are actually the same length

 We see in 2D, not 3D

Light rays enter the eye through the cornea and lens. The lens focuses an image on the retina. On the retina it is always a two-dimensional representation, even if it is a three-dimensional object. This image is sent to the visual cortex in the brain, and that's where recognition of patterns takes place, for example, "Oh, I recognize that as a door." The visual cortex turns the 2D image into a 3D representation.

The visual cortex puts all the information together

According to John Medina (2009), the retina receives electrical patterns from what we look at and creates several tracks from the patterns. Some tracks contain information about shadows, others about movement, and so on. As many as 12 tracks of information are then sent to the brain's visual cortex. There, different regions respond to and process the information. For example, one area responds only to lines that are tilted to 40 degrees, another only to color, another only to motion, and another only to edges. Eventually all of these data get combined into just two tracks: one for movement (is the object moving?) and another for location (where is this object in relation to me?).

Takeaways

＊ What you think people are going to see on your Web page may not be what they do see. It might depend on their background, knowledge, familiarity with what they are looking at, and expectations.

＊ You might be able to persuade people to see things in a certain way, depending on how they are presented.

---

2 PERIPHERAL VISION IS USED MORE THAN CENTRAL VISION TO GET THE GIST OF WHAT YOU SEE

You have two types of vision: central and peripheral. Central vision is what you use to look at things directly and to see details. Peripheral vision encompasses the rest of the visual field—areas that are visible, but that you're not looking at directly. Being able to see things out of the corner of your eye is certainly useful, but new research from Kansas State University shows that peripheral vision is more important in understanding the world around us than most people realize. It seems that we get information on what type of scene we're looking at from our peripheral vision.

 Why blinking on a screen is so annoying

People can't help but notice movement in their peripheral vision. For example, if you're reading text on a computer screen, and there's some animation or something blinking off to the side, you can't help but look at it. This can be quite annoying if you're trying to concentrate on reading the text in front of you. This is peripheral vision at work! This is why advertisers use blinking and flashing in the ads that are at the periphery of web pages. Even though we may find it annoying, it does get our attention.

Adam Larson and Lester Loschky (2009) showed people photographs of common scenes, such as a kitchen or a living room. In some of the photographs the outside of the image was obscured, and in others the central part of the image was obscured. The images were shown for very short amounts of time, and were purposely shown with a gray filter so they were somewhat hard to see (see **Figure 2.1** and **Figure 2.2**). Then they asked the research participants to identify what they were looking at.

Larson and Loschky found that if the central part of the photo was missing, people could still identify what they were looking at. But when the peripheral part of the image was missing, then they couldn't say whether the scene was a living room or a kitchen. They tried obscuring different amounts of the photo. They concluded that central vision is the most critical for specific object recognition, but peripheral vision is used for getting the gist of a scene.

FIGURE 2.1 A central vision photo used in Larson and Loschky research

FIGURE 2.2 A peripheral vision photo used in Larson and Loschky research

 Peripheral vision kept our ancestors alive on the savannah

The theory, from an evolutionary standpoint, is that early humans who were sharpening their flint, or looking up at the clouds, and yet still noticed that a lion was coming at them in their peripheral vision survived to pass on their genes. Those with poor peripheral vision didn't survive to pass on genes.

Recent research confirms this idea. Dimitri Bayle (2009) placed pictures of fearful objects in subjects' peripheral vision or central vision. Then he measured how long it took for the amygdala (the emotional part of the brain that responds to fearful images) to react. When the fearful object was shown in the central vision, it took between 140 to 190 milliseconds for the amygdala to react. But when objects were shown in peripheral vision, it only took 80 milliseconds for the amygdala to react.

Takeaways

* People use peripheral vision when they look at a computer screen, and usually decide what a page is about based on a quick glimpse of what is in their peripheral vision.

* Although the middle of the screen is important for central vision, don't ignore what is in the viewers' peripheral vision. Make sure the information in the periphery communicates clearly the purpose of the page and the site.

* If you want users to concentrate on a certain part of the screen, don't put animation or blinking elements in their peripheral vision.

3 PEOPLE IDENTIFY OBJECTS BY RECOGNIZING PATTERNS

Recognizing patterns helps you make quick sense of the sensory input that comes to you every second. Your eyes and brain want to create patterns, even if there are no real patterns there. In **Figure 3.1**, you probably see four sets of two dots each rather than eight individual dots. You interpret the white space, or lack of it, as a pattern.

FIGURE 3.1 Your brain wants to see patterns

⭐ Individual cells respond to certain shapes

In 1959 David Hubel and Torsten Wiesel showed that some cells in the visual cortex respond only to horizontal lines, others respond only to vertical lines, others respond only to edges, and still others respond only to certain angles.

THE GEON THEORY OF OBJECT RECOGNITION

There have been many theories over the years about how we see and recognize objects. An early theory was that the brain has a memory bank that stores millions of objects, and when you see an object, you compare it with all the items in your memory bank until you find the one that matches. But research now suggests that you recognize basic shapes in what you are looking at, and use these basic shapes, called geometric icons (or geons), to identify objects. Irving Biederman came up with the idea of geons in 1985 (**Figure 3.2**). It's thought that there are 24 basic shapes that we recognize; they form the building blocks of all the objects we see and identify.

The visual cortex is more active when you are imagining

The visual cortex is more active when you are imagining something than when you are actually perceiving it (Solso, 2005). Activity occurs in the same location in the visual cortex, but there is more activity when we imagine. The theory is that the visual cortex has to work harder since the stimulus is not actually present.

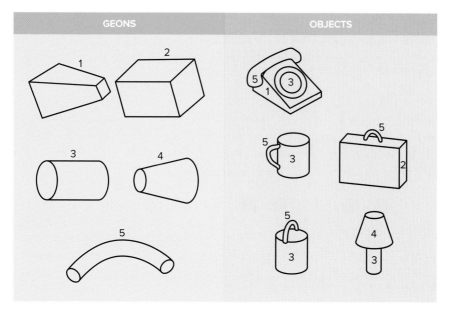

FIGURE 3.2 Some samples of Biederman's geons

Takeaways

∗ Use patterns as much as possible, since people will automatically be looking for them. Use grouping and white space to create patterns.

∗ If you want people to recognize an object (for example, an icon), use a simple geometric drawing of the object. This will make it easier to recognize the underlying geons, and thus make the object easier and faster to recognize.

∗ Favor 2D elements over 3D ones. The eyes communicate what they see to the brain as a 2D object. 3D representations on the screen may actually slow down recognition and comprehension.

4 THERE'S A SPECIAL PART OF THE BRAIN JUST FOR RECOGNIZING FACES

Imagine that you're walking down a busy street in a large city when you suddenly see the face of a family member. Even if you were not expecting to see this person, and even if there are dozens, or even hundreds, of people in your visual field, you will immediately recognize him or her as your relative. You'll also have an accompanying emotional response, be it love, hate, fear, or otherwise.

Although the visual cortex is huge and takes up significant brain resources, there is a special part of the brain outside the visual cortex whose sole purpose is to recognize faces. Identified by Nancy Kanwisher (1997), the fusiform face area (FFA) allows faces to bypass the brain's usual interpretive channels and helps us identify them more quickly than objects. The FFA is also near the amygdala, the brain's emotional center.

 People with autism don't view faces with the FFA

Research by Karen Pierce (2001) showed that people with autism don't use the FFA when looking at faces. Instead, they use other, regular pathways in the brain and visual cortex that are normally used to recognize and interpret objects but not faces.

 We look where the face looks

Eye-tracking research shows that if a picture of a face looks away from us and toward a product on a Web page (see **Figure 4.1**), then we tend to also look at the product.

But remember, just because people look at something doesn't mean they're paying attention. As you consider your Web approach, you'll have to decide whether you want to establish an emotional connection (the face looking right at the user) or direct attention (the face looking directly at a product).

FIGURE 4.1 We look where the person looks

People are born with a preference for faces

Research by Catherine Mondloch et al. (1999) shows that newborns less than an hour old prefer looking at something that has facial features.

 The eyes have it: people decide who and what is alive by looking at the eyes

Christine Looser and T. Wheatley (2010) takes pictures of people and then morphs them in stages into inanimate mannequin faces. She shows the stages and has research subjects decide when the picture is no longer a human and alive. **Figure 4.2** shows examples of her pictures. Looser's research found that subjects say the pictures no longer show someone who is alive at about the 75 percent mark. She also found that people primarily use the eyes to decide if a picture shows someone who is human and alive.

FIGURE 4.2 An example of Looser's and Wheatley's people to mannequin faces

Takeaways

* People recognize and react to faces on Web pages faster than anything else on the page (at least by those who are not autistic).

* Faces looking right at people will have the greatest emotional impact on a Web page, probably because the eyes are the most important part of the face.

* If a face on a Web page looks at another spot or product on the page, people will also tend to look at that product. This doesn't necessarily mean that they paid attention to it, just that they physically looked at it.

5 PEOPLE IMAGINE OBJECTS TILTED AND AT A SLIGHT ANGLE ABOVE

If you ask someone to draw a picture of a coffee cup, chances are they'll draw something that looks something like **Figure 5.1**.

FIGURE 5.1 How we "see" objects in our heads

In fact, Stephen Palmer (1981) traveled around the world and asked people to draw a coffee cup. **Figure 5.2** shows examples of what they drew.

FIGURE 5.2 What most people drew when asked to draw a coffee cup

What's interesting about these drawings is the angle and perspective. A few of the cups are sketched straight on, but most are drawn from a perspective slightly above the cup looking down, and offset a little to the right or left. This has been dubbed the *canonical perspective*. Very few people would draw a coffee cup as in **Figure 5.3**, which is what you'd see if you were looking at a coffee cup from above.

Of course not, you say, but...*why not?* You might argue that the first perspective is the one that you actually see most of the time when you look at a coffee cup, but I will tell you that this research has been done on many objects, and people most quickly recognized them all at this same canonical perspective, even though they don't look at all of these objects from above most of the time. The research asked people to identify various animals, such as a very small dog or cat. The canonical perspective still won out, even though we most often see cats or very small dogs from high above, not just slightly above (unless you crawl around on the ground a lot). It seems to be a universal trait that we think about, remember, imagine, and recognize objects from this canonical perspective.

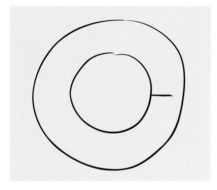

FIGURE 5.3 Most people don't draw a coffee cup like this

Takeaways

* People recognize a drawing or object faster and remember it better if it's shown in the canonical perspective.

* If you have icons at your Web site or in your Web or software application, draw them from a canonical perspective.

6 PEOPLE SCAN SCREENS BASED ON PAST EXPERIENCE AND EXPECTATIONS

Where do people look first on a computer screen? Where do they look next? It depends partially on what they're doing and expecting. If they read in a language that moves from left to right, then they tend to look at the screen from left to right. If they read from right to left, it is the opposite. However, they don't start in the topmost corner. Because people have gotten used to the idea that there are things on computer screens that are less relevant to the task at hand, such as logos, blank space, and navigation bars (see **Figure 6.1**), they tend to look at the center of the screen and avoid the edges.

People don't look at screen edges

People consider the point where the meaningful informaton begins to be the true "top left"

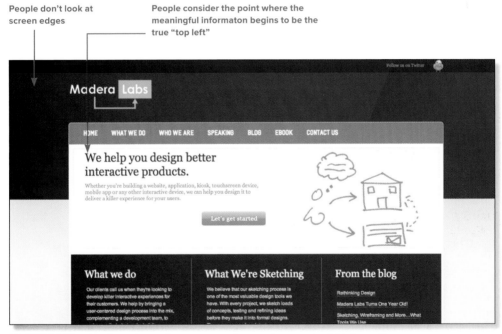

FIGURE 6.1 We skip the edges of a screen and move to meaningful information

After a first glance at a screen, people move in their culture's normal reading pattern (left to right, right to left, top to bottom). If something grabs their attention, for example, a large photo (especially one with someone's face) or movement (an animated banner or video) somewhere else on the screen, then you can pull them away from this normal tendency.

PEOPLE HAVE A MENTAL MODEL OF WHAT THEY WANT TO SEE AND WHERE THEY WANT TO SEE IT

People have a mental model of where things tend to be on computer screens, and a mental model for particular applications or Web sites that they use. They tend to look at a screen based on these mental models. For example, if they shop at Amazon a lot and use the search field, they'll likely look right at the search field when the screen loads.

IF THERE IS A PROBLEM, PEOPLE NARROW THEIR VIEW

If there is an error or unexpected problem with the task people are trying to accomplish, then they stop looking at other parts of the screen and focus on the problem area. We'll discuss this more in the "People Make Mistakes" chapter.

Takeaways

* Put the most important information (or things you want people to focus on) in the top third of the screen or in the middle.

* Avoid putting anything important at the edges, since people tend not to look there.

* Design the screen or page so that people can move in their normal reading pattern. Avoid a pattern where people have to bounce back and forth to many parts of the screen to accomplish a task.

7 PEOPLE SEE CUES THAT TELL THEM WHAT TO DO WITH AN OBJECT

You've probably had the experience of encountering a door handle that doesn't work the way it should: the handle looks like you should pull, but in fact you need to push. In the real world, objects communicate to you about how you can, and should, interact with them. For example, by their size and shape, doorknobs invite you to grab and turn them. The handle on a coffee mug tells you to curl a few fingers through it and lift it up. A pair of scissors invites you to put fingers through the circles and move your thumb up and down to open and close. If the item, like the door handle, gives you cues that don't work, you get annoyed and frustrated. These cues are called *affordances*.

James Gibson wrote about the idea of affordance in 1979. He described affordances as *action possibilities* in the environment. In 1988 Don Norman modified the idea of affordances in his book *The Design of Everyday Things*. He referred to the idea of *perceived* affordances: if you want people to take action on an object, whether in real life or on a computer screen, you need to make sure that they can easily perceive, figure out, and interpret what the object is and what they can and should do with it.

When you try to accomplish a task, such as opening a door to a room or ordering a book at a Web site, you automatically, and largely unconsciously, look around you to find objects and tools to help you. If you are the one designing the environment for the task, make sure that the objects in the environment are easy to see, easy to find, and have clear affordances.

Take a look at the door handle in **Figure 7.1**. Because of its shape, you'll tend to grab it and pull down. If that's the way it works, then you'd say that the door handle is well designed and that it has a clear perceived affordance.

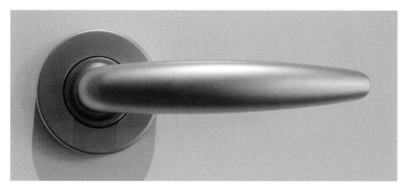

FIGURE 7.1 This door handle invites you to grab and pull down

Figure 7.2 shows a handle shaped in a way that invites you to grab and pull, but the PUSH sign indicates the door simply doesn't work that way. That's known as *incorrect affordance*.

FIGURE 7.2 This door handle reads *PUSH* but its design encourages you to pull

PERCEIVED AFFORDANCES ON COMPUTER SCREENS

When you're designing an application or Web site, think about the affordances of objects on the screen. For example, have you ever wondered what makes people want to click on a button? Cues in the button's shadow tell people that it can be pushed in, the way a button on an actual device can be pushed in.

Figure 7.3 shows a button on a remote control. The shape and shadows give you cues that encourage you to press the button to activate it.

FIGURE 7.3 Buttons on physical devices have shadows that make you want to press them

You can simulate these shadows online, too. In **Figure 7.4**, shadows of different colors around the edges make the button look pushed in. Try turning the book upside down and looking at the same button. Now it will look like it's not pushed in, and the shadows will give cues to push the button.

FIGURE 7.4 This button looks pushed in, but turn the book upside down and see what happens

These visual cues are subtle, but they are important. Many buttons on Web sites have some of these visual cues, such as the button in **Figure 7.5**, but lately Web sites are losing the cues. In **Figure 7.6**, the button is just text in a colored square.

FIGURE 7.5 The use of shading makes this look like a button

FIGURE 7.6 Online buttons are losing their cues

HYPERLINKS ARE LOSING THEIR AFFORDANCE CUES

Most people have figured out the affordance cue that blue, underlined text means that the text is hyperlinked, and if you click on it you will go to a different page. But lately many hyperlinks are more subtle, with the only cue that they are clickable showing up when you hover. **Figure 7.7** shows what the New York Times Reader page looks like before you hover, and **Figure 7.8** shows what it looks like when you hover. It takes an extra step to see the cues. And if you are reading on your iPad, all of these cues are missing. You can't hover with your finger on an iPad. By the time you've touched the screen with your finger, you've clicked on the link.

G.O.P. Sets Up Huge Target for Budget Ax

BY JACKIE CALMES

Republicans are moving to make good on a promise to cut $100 billion in domestic spending this year.

DEALBOOK

Facebook Deal Offers Freedom From Scrutiny

BY MIGUEL HELFT

Flush with cash, Facebook may be able to delay an initial public offering of stock and remain free of government regulation.

FIGURE 7.7 Times Reader showing no initial affordance cues

G.O.P. Sets Up Huge Target for Budget Ax

BY JACKIE CALMES

Republicans are moving to make good on a promise to cut $100 billion in domestic spending this year.

DEALBOOK

Facebook Deal Offers Freedom From Scrutiny

BY MIGUEL HELFT

Flush with cash, Facebook may be able to delay an initial public offering of stock and remain free of government regulation.

FIGURE 7.8 In Times Reader, affordance cues show up when you hover

Takeaways

✳ Think about affordance cues when you design. By giving people cues about what they can do with a particular object, you make it more likely that they will take that action.

✳ Use shading to show when an object is chosen or active.

✳ Avoid providing incorrect affordance cues.

✳ Rethink hover cues if you're designing for a device that uses touch rather than a pointing device.

8 PEOPLE CAN MISS CHANGES IN THEIR VISUAL FIELDS

⭐ **Spoiler Alert**

If you haven't seen what is famously called the "Gorilla video," then you should check this out now. Go to my blog:

http://www.whatmakesthemclick.net/2009/10/25/100-things-you-should-know-about-people-1-inattention-blindness/

Take the test. If you don't do this now, then I'm going to spoil the effect for you below as I discuss the video.

The "Gorilla video" is an example of *inattention blindness* or *change blindness*. The idea is that people often miss large changes in their visual fields. This has been shown in many experiments, although the basketball/gorilla experiment is the most well known. (Videos from some of the other experiments are at my blog at the URL above.)

In their book, *The Invisible Gorilla*, Christopher Chabris and Daniel Simons (2010) describe additional research they did with eye-tracking equipment. Eye tracking is a technology that can track where someone is looking. More specifically, it tracks where the foveal or central gaze is. It doesn't track peripheral vision. Eye-tracking research done while people are watching the basketball/gorilla video shows that everyone watching the video "sees" the gorilla in the video, meaning that their eyes are looking at the gorilla, but only 50 percent are aware that they have seen the gorilla. Chabris and Simons have conducted many studies on this phenomenon, and they have concluded that if you are paying attention to one thing, and you don't expect changes to appear, then you can easily miss changes that do occur.

 Eye-tracking data can be misleading

Eye tracking is a technology that allows you to see and record what a person is looking at, in what order, and for how long. It is often used to study Web sites to see where people are looking, including where they look first, second, and so on. One of its benefits is that you don't have to rely on what people *say* they are looking at, but instead you can collect the data directly. But eye-tracking data can be misleading for several reasons: 1) As we've discussed in this section, eye tracking tells you what people looked at, but that doesn't mean that they paid attention to it. 2) The Larson and Loschky research in this chapter tells us that peripheral vision is just as important as central vision. Eye tracking measures only central vision. 3) Early eye-tracking research by Alfred Yarbus (1967) showed that what people look at depends on what questions they are asked while they are looking. It's therefore easy to accidently skew the eye-tracking data depending on what instructions you give them before and during the eye tracking study.

Takeaways

* Don't assume that people will see something on a computer screen just because it's there. This is especially true when you refresh a screen and make one change on it. Users may not even realize they are even looking at a different screen.

* If you want to be sure that people notice a change in their visual fields, add additional visual cues (such as blinking) or auditory cues (such as a beep).

* Be cautious about how you interpret eye-tracking data. Don't ascribe too much importance to it or use it as the main basis for design decisions.

9 PEOPLE BELIEVE THAT THINGS THAT ARE CLOSE TOGETHER BELONG TOGETHER

If two items are near each other (a photo and text for example), then people assume they go together. This connection is strongest for items that are together left to right. In **Figure 9.1**, the photo goes with the text below it. But because we read left to right, and because there is very little space between the photo and the text to the right, we may expect that the photo and the text to the right belong together.

FIGURE 9.1 You might assume that this photo belongs with the text to the right because they are close together and we read from left to right. But in this example, the photo actually goes with the text below it—and that will be confusing to most readers.

Takeaways

* If you want items (pictures, photos, headings, or text) to be seen as belonging together, then put them in close proximity.

* Before you use lines or boxes to separate items or group them together, try experimenting with the amount of space between them first. Sometimes changing the spacing is sufficient, and you'll be reducing the visual noise of the page.

* Put more space between items that don't go together and less space between items that do. This sounds like common sense, but many Web page layouts ignore this idea.

10 RED AND BLUE TOGETHER ARE HARD ON THE EYES

When lines or text of different colors are projected or printed, the depths of the lines may appear to be different. One color may jump out while another color appears recessed. This effect is called *chromostereopsis*. The effect is strongest with red and blue, but it can also happen with other colors, for example, red and green. These color combinations can be hard and tiring to look at or read. **Figure 10.1** shows some examples of chromostereopsis.

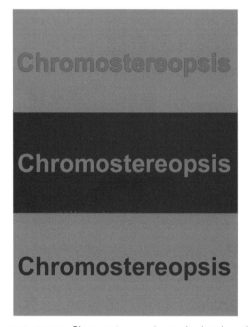

FIGURE 10.1 Chromostereopsis can be hard on the eyes

Takeaways

* Avoid putting blue and red or green and red near each other on a page or screen.

* Avoid blue or green text on a red background, and red or green text on a blue background.

11 NINE PERCENT OF MEN AND ONE-HALF PERCENT OF WOMEN ARE COLOR-BLIND

The term color blindness is actually a misnomer. Most people who are "color-blind" are not blind to all colors, but really have a color deficiency that makes it hard for them to see differences between some colors. Most color blindness is hereditary, although some can be acquired through disease or injury. Most of the color genes are on the X chromosome. Since men have only one X chromosome and women have two, men are more likely to have problems with color vision than women.

There are many different kinds of color blindness, but the most common is a difficulty distinguishing between reds, yellows, and greens. This is called "red-green" color blindness. Other forms, such as problems distinguishing blues from yellows, or where everything looks gray, are very rare.

Figure 11.1 shows a map of winter driving conditions from the Wisconsin Department of Transportation's Web site as it appears to someone who has no color blindness. **Figure 11.2** shows the same page as a person with red-green color blindness would see it, and **Figure 11.3** shows the same page as a person with blue-yellow color deficiency would see it. Notice that the colors are different.

The rule of thumb is that wherever you use color to give specific meaning, you need a redundant coding scheme, for example, color *and* line thickness, so that people who are color-blind will be able to decipher the code without needing to see specific colors.

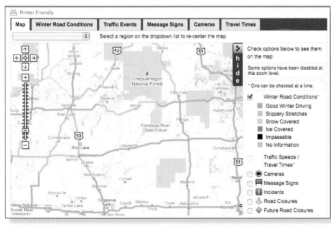

FIGURE 11.1 Full-color vision

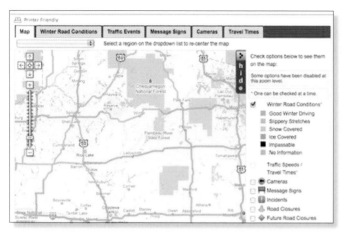

FIGURE 11.2 Red-green color deficiency

FIGURE 11.3 Blue-yellow color deficiency

Another approach is to pick a color scheme that works for people who have the various types of color blindness. **Figure 11.4**, **Figure 11.5**, and **Figure 11.6** are from a Web site that shows the spread of influenza for a particular week. At this site they have purposely picked colors that look the same for people regardless of the type of color blindness they have, and even if they are not color-blind. The three instances of the Web page look almost exactly the same.

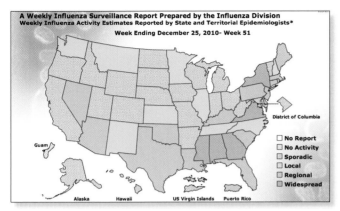

FIGURE 11.4 Full-color vision (WWW.CDC.GOV)

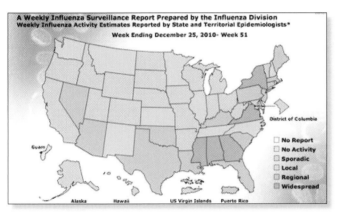

FIGURE 11.5 Red-green color deficiency (WWW.CDC.GOV)

FIGURE 11.6 Blue-yellow color deficiency (WWW.CDC.GOV)

Use Web sites to check for color blindness effects

There are several sites you can use to check how your images or Web site will appear to someone who has color blindness. Here are two I recommend:

www.vischeck.com

colorfilter.wickline.org

 Those who are color-blind can often see camouflage better

Some say it is because they are not distracted by color, while others say it is because those who are color-blind are used to looking for pattern, texture, or other cues. Regardless of the reason, some color-blind individuals can see camouflage better than those who have full-color vision.

Takeaways

* Check your images and Web sites with www.vischeck.com or colorfilter.wickline.org to see how they will look to someone who is color-blind.

* If you use color to imply a certain meaning (for example, items in green need immediate attention), use a redundant coding scheme (items in green and with a box around them need immediate attention).

* When designing color coding, consider colors that work for everyone, for example, varying shades of brown and yellow. Avoid red, green, and blue.

12 THE MEANINGS OF COLORS VARY BY CULTURE

Many years ago I worked with a client who had created a color map of the different business regions for their company, showing the total revenue for the quarter for each region. Yellow was for the eastern part of the U.S., green for the central states, and red for the western states. The VP of Sales got to the podium and started his slide show to the financial and accounting staff of the company. Up came the colored map and a gasp could be heard in the auditorium, followed by the buzz of urgent conversation. The VP tried to continue his talk, but he had lost everyone's attention. They were all talking amongst themselves.

Finally someone blurted out, "What the heck is going on in the West?"

"What do you mean?" the VP asked. "Nothing is going on. They had a great quarter."

To an accountant or financial person, red is a bad thing. It means that they are losing money. The presenter had to explain that he had just randomly picked red.

Colors have associations and meanings, for example, red means "in the red" or financial trouble, or it could mean danger or stop. Green means money or "go." Pick colors carefully since they have these meanings. And different colors might mean different things to subgroups.

If you are designing for people in different parts of the world, then you have to also consider the color meanings in other cultures. A few colors have similar meanings everywhere (gold, for example, stands for success and high quality in most cultures), but most colors have different meanings in different cultures. For example, in the U.S. white signifies purity and is used at weddings, but in other cultures white is the color used for death and funerals. Happiness is associated with white, green, yellow, or red, depending on the part of the world you are in.

 Check out the David McCandless Color Wheel

David McCandless of InformationIsBeautiful.net has a color wheel that shows how different colors are viewed by different cultures: http://www.informationisbeautiful.net/visualizations/colours-in-cultures/

Research on color and moods

Research shows that colors affect mood. The restaurant and hospitality industry has studied this a lot. For example, in the U.S. orange makes people agitated, so they won't stay long (useful in fast food restaurants). Browns and blues are soothing, so people will stay (useful in bars). However, in order for a color to affect mood, the person has to be sitting in a room surrounded by that color. The effect does not seem to work if he or she is simply looking at a computer screen that has a particular color on it.

Takeaways

✳ Choose your colors carefully, taking into account the meaning that the colors may invoke.

✳ Pick a few major cultures or countries that you will be reaching with your design and check them on the cultural color chart from InformationIsBeautiful.net to be sure you're avoiding unintended color associations for that culture.

HOW
PEOPLE
READ

With adult literacy rates now over 80 percent worldwide, reading is a primary form of communication for most people. But *how* do we read? And what should designers know about reading?

13 IT'S A MYTH THAT CAPITAL LETTERS ARE INHERENTLY HARD TO READ

You've probably heard that words in uppercase letters are harder to read than those in mixed case or lowercase. You've probably even heard some kind of percentage cited, such as "between 14 and 20 percent harder." The story goes that we read by recognizing the shapes of words and groups of words. Words in mixed case or lowercase letters have unique shapes. Words in all capital letters have the same shape—a rectangle of a certain size—so, in theory, they're harder to distinguish (**Figure 13.1**).

FIGURE 13.1 The word shape theory

This explanation sounds plausible, but it's not really accurate. There's no research showing that the shapes of words help us read more accurately or more quickly. A psycholinguist named James Cattell came up with that idea in 1886. There was some evidence for it then, but more recent work by Kenneth Paap (1984) and Keith Rayner (1998) has revealed that what we're actually doing when we read is recognizing and anticipating letters. And then, based on the letters, we recognize the word. Let's look more closely at how we read.

READING ISN'T AS FLUID AS IT SEEMS

When we read, we have the impression that our eyes are moving smoothly across the page, but that's not what's actually happening. Our eyes move in quick, sharp jumps, with short periods of stillness in between. The jumps are called saccades (about seven to nine letters at a time) and the moments of stillness are called fixations (about 250 milliseconds long). During the saccades, we can't see anything—we're essentially blind—but the movements are so fast that we don't even realize they're happening. Our eyes look forward during most of the saccades, but they look backward 10 to 15 percent of the time, rereading letters and words.

Figure 13.2 shows an example of the saccade and fixation pattern. The black dots are the fixations and the curved lines are the saccade movements.

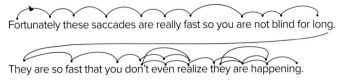

Fortunately these saccades are really fast so you are not blind for long.

They are so fast that you don't even realize they are happening.

FIGURE 13.2 An example of a saccade and fixation pattern

 We use peripheral vision when we read

A saccade spans about seven to nine letters, but our perceptual span is actually double that. In 1996, Kenneth Goodman found that we use peripheral vision to see what comes next when we read. We read ahead about 15 letters at a time, viewing the characters to the right (assuming we're reading left to right), although now and then a saccade jumps us backward and we reread a group of letters. Although we read ahead about 15 letters at a time, we only get the meaning for part of that span. We pick up the semantic cues of letters 1 through 7, but merely recognize letters 8 through 15.

 Reading music is similar to reading text

People who read music fluently use the same saccades, fixations, and reading ahead of 15 "letters" that they do when reading text.

SO, IS ALL CAPITALS HARDER TO READ THEN?

We *do* actually read uppercase letters more slowly, but only because we don't see them as often. Most of what we read is in mixed case, so we're used to it. If you practice reading text in all capital letters, you'll eventually read that text as fast as you read mixed case. This doesn't mean you should start using capital letters for all your text. Since peole are unused to reading that way, it will slow them down. And these days, text in all caps is perceived as "shouting" (**Figure 13.3**).

*DOUBLE CHECK THE LOCATION YOU ARE SIGNING UP FOR
*BE SURE TO ASSIGN AND UNDO CODE (Codes are case sensitive)
*CHECK YOUR EMAIL FREQUENTLY - CLASS INFO WILL BE COMMUNICATED VIA EMAIL

FIGURE 13.3 We perceive uppercase letters as shouting, but they aren't inherently harder to read

A Good Summary Of The Research On Uppercase

Kevin Larson wrote a great article summarizing the research on uppercase versus mixed case:

http://www.microsoft.com/typography/ctfonts/wordrecognition.aspx

Takeaways

✳ People perceive all capitals as shouting, and they're unused to reading them, so use all uppercase sparingly.

✳ Save all capital letters for headlines, and when you need to get someone's attention, for example, before deleting an important file.

14 READING AND COMPREHENDING ARE TWO DIFFERENT THINGS

If you're a biologist, then this paragraph might make sense right away:

The regulation of the TCA cycle is largely determined by substrate availability and product inhibition. NADH, a product of all of the dehydrogenases in the TCA cycle, with the exception of succinate dehydrogenase, inhibits pyruvate dehydrogenase, isocitrate dehydrogenase, a-ketoglutarate dehydrogenase, while succinyl-CoA inhibits succinyl-CoA synthetase and citrate synthase.

If you're not a biologist, then it might take you a long time to understand what that paragraph says. You can read the paragraph, but that doesn't mean you understand it. New information is assimilated more thoroughly when it is plugged into existing cognitive structures.

 You can calculate the readability of your text

The Flesch-Kincaid formula is commonly used to calculate the readability of text. It provides both a reading ease score and a reading grade-level score. The higher the scores, the easier the passage is to read. Low scores mean the passage is hard to read. The formula is shown in **Figure 14.1**.

$$206.835 - 1.015 \left(\frac{\text{total words}}{\text{total sentences}} \right) - 84.6 \left(\frac{\text{total syllables}}{\text{total words}} \right)$$

FIGURE 14.1 The Flesch-Kincaid Readability Formula

CAN YOU READ THIS PARAGRAPH?

Eevn touhgh the wrosd are srcmaelbd, cahnecs are taht you can raed tihs praagarph aynawy. The order of the ltteers in each word is not vrey ipmrotnat. But the frsit and lsat ltteer msut be in the rhgit psotitoin. The ohter ltetres can be all mxeid up and you can sitll raed whtiuot a lot of porbelms. This is bceusae radenig is all aobut atciniptanig the nxet word.

When you read you don't absorb exact letters and words and then interpret them later. You anticipate what will come next. The more previous knowledge you have, the easier it is to anticipate and interpret.

Some word processing software has the Flesch-Kincaid formula built in. Or you can use this online tool to calculate the reading level of a particular passage:

http://www.standards-schmandards.com/exhibits/rix/index.php

I tested a paragraph from one of my blog articles (www.whatmakesthemclick.net). The results are shown in **Figure 14.2.**

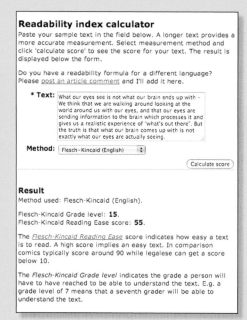

FIGURE 14.2 An example of readability score results from one of my blog articles

TITLES AND HEADLINES ARE CRITICAL

Read this paragraph:

First you sort the items into like categories. Using color for sorting is common, but you can also use other characteristics, such as texture or type of handling needed. Once you have sorted the items, you are ready to use the equipment. You want to process each category from the sorting separately. Place one category in the machine at a time.

What is the paragraph about? It's hard to understand. But what if I give you the same paragraph with a title:

Using your new washing machine

First you sort the items into like categories. Using color for sorting is common, but you can also use other characteristics, such as texture or type of handling needed. Once you have sorted the items, you are ready to use the equipment. You want to process each category from the sorting separately. Place one category in the machine at a time.

The paragraph is still poorly written, but now at least it is understandable.

 People use different parts of the brain to process words

Words are processed in different parts of the brain depending on what you're doing with them. Viewing or reading words, listening, speaking, generating verbs—all of these word activities engage different parts of the brain, as shown in **Figure 14.3**.

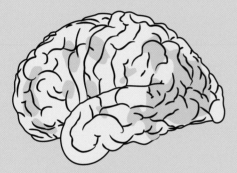
Passively viewing words

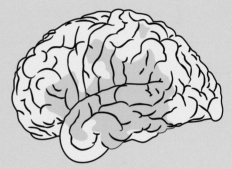
Listening to words

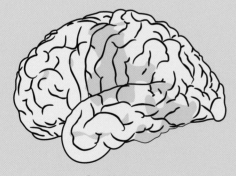
Speaking words

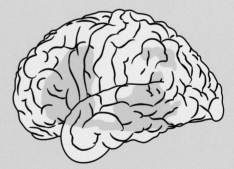
Generating verbs

FIGURE 14.3 Different parts of the brain process words

WHAT YOU REMEMBER OF WHAT YOU READ DEPENDS ON YOUR POINT OF VIEW

In a study by Anderson and Pichert (1978), people read a story about a house and the contents within the house. One group was told to read the story from a buyer's standpoint, and another group was told to read the story from a burglar's point of view. The information they remembered after reading the story differed depending on their viewpoint.

Takeaways

* People are active readers. What they understand and remember from what they read depends on their previous experience, their point of view while reading, and the instructions they are given beforehand.

* Don't assume that people will remember specific information in what they read.

* Provide a meaningful title or headline. It's one of the most important things you can do.

* Tailor the reading level of your text to your audience. Use simple words and fewer syllables to make your material accessible to a wider audience.

15 PATTERN RECOGNITION HELPS PEOPLE IDENTIFY LETTERS IN DIFFERENT FONTS

People have been debating which fonts are better, easier to read, or most appropriate for centuries. One such debate centers around the use of two types of fonts: serif versus sans serif. Some argue that sans serif typefaces are easier to read because they are plain; others contend that serif fonts are easier to read because the serifs draw the eye toward the next letter. In fact, research shows no difference in comprehension, reading speed, or preference between serif and sans serif fonts.

 People identify letters through pattern recognition

How is it that you can recognize all of the marks in **Figure 15.1** as the letter *A*?

FIGURE 15.1 We can recognize many variations of a letter

You haven't memorized all of these versions of the letter *A*. Instead you've formed a memory pattern of what an *A* looks like. When you see something similar, your brain recognizes the pattern. (See the discussion of geons in the chapter called "How We See" for more information about how we recognize shapes.)

Designers use fonts to evoke a mood, brand, or association. Some font families invoke a time period (old fashioned versus modern), while others convey seriousness or playfulness. In terms of readability, however, the font you choose is not critical as long as it is not so decorative as to make it hard to identify the letters; some fonts interfere with the brain's ability to recognize patterns.

Figure 15.2 shows different decorative fonts. The first font is relatively easy to read; the others become progressively more difficult. They make it hard for the brain to recognize the patterns of the letters.

There are many fonts that are easy to read. Any of them are fine to use. But avoid a font that is so decorative that it starts to interfere with pattern recognition in the brain.

There are many fonts that are easy to read. Any of them are fine to use. But avoid a font that is so decorative that it starts to interfere with pattern recognition in the brain.

There are many fonts that are easy to read. Any of them are fine to use. But avoid a font that is so decorative that it starts to interfere with pattern recognition in the brain.

There are many fonts that are easy to read. Any of them are fine to use. But avoid a font that is so decorative that it starts to interfere with pattern recognition in the brain.

FIGURE 15.2 Some decorative fonts are readable, but others are less so

 Learn more about font type, typography, and readability

If you're interested in reading the research about font type, typography, and readability, check out this great Web site:

http://www.alexpoole.info/academic/literaturereview.html

IF A FONT IS HARD TO READ, THE MEANING OF THE TEXT WILL BE LOST

Hyunjin Song and Norbert Schwarz (2008) gave people written instructions on how to do a physical exercise. If the instructions were in an easy-to-read font (such as Arial), people estimated that it would take about eight minutes to do the exercise and that it wouldn't be too difficult. They were willing to incorporate the exercise into their daily workout. But if the instructions were given in an overly decorative font (such as Brush

Script MT Italic), people estimated it would take almost twice as long—15 minutes—to do the exercise, and they rated the exercise as being difficult to do (**Figure 15.3**). They were also less likely to be willing to incorporate it into their routine.

Tuck your chin into your chest, and then lift your chin upward as far as possible. 6-10 repetitions.
Lower your left ear toward your left shoulder and then your right ear toward your right shoulder. 6-10 repetitions.

Tuck your chin into your chest, and then lift your chin upward as far as possible. 6-10 repetitions.
Lower your left ear toward your left shoulder and then your right ear toward your right shoulder. 6-10 repetitions.

FIGURE 15.3 If the text used for instructions is hard to read, as it is in the second text sample, the reader likewise will think the instructions are hard to do

Takeaways

＊ Serif and sans serif fonts are equal in terms of readability.

＊ Unusual or overly decorative fonts can interfere with pattern recognition and slow down reading.

＊ If people have trouble reading the font, they will transfer that feeling of difficulty to the meaning of the text itself and decide that the subject of the text is hard to do or understand.

16 FONT SIZE MATTERS

When it comes to fonts, size matters a lot. The font size needs to be big enough for users to read the text without strain. And it's not just older individuals who need fonts to be bigger—young people also complain when font sizes are too small to read.

Some fonts can be the same size, but look bigger, due to the x-height. The x-height is literally the height of the small letter x in the font family. Different fonts have different x-heights, and as a result, some fonts look larger than others, even though they are the same point size.

Figure 16.1 shows how the font size and x-heights are measured.

FIGURE 16.1 How font size and x-height are measured

Some newer font families, such as Tahoma and Verdana, have been designed with large x-heights so they are easier to read on a screen. **Figure 16.2** shows different font families that are all the same point size. Some look bigger, however, because of their larger x-height.

All the fonts in this illustration are the same size, but some look larger than others because the x-height of different font families vary. This one is Arial.

All the fonts in this illustration are the same size, but some look larger than others because the x-height of different font families vary. This one is Times New Roman.

All the fonts in this illustration are the same size, but some look larger than others because the x-height of different font families vary. This one is Verdana.

All the fonts in this illustration are the same size, but some look larger than others because the x-height of different font families vary. This one is Tahoma.

FIGURE 16.2 Large x-heights can make a font look larger

Takeaways

* Choose a point size that is large enough for people of various ages to read comfortably.

* Use a font with a large x-height for online viewing so that the type will appear to be larger.

17 READING A COMPUTER SCREEN IS HARDER THAN READING PAPER

Computer screens, Kindles, and paper create different reading experiences. When you read on a computer screen, the image is not stable—it is being refreshed constantly, and the screen is emitting light. When you read text on paper the image is stable (not being refreshed), and instead of emitting light the paper is reflecting light. The refreshing of the image and emitting of the light on the computer display are tiring on the eyes. Electronic ink (as in the Kindle) mimics the appearance of ink on paper. It reflects light and holds the text stable without refreshing.

To make text on a computer screen easier to read, make sure you use a large enough font and create enough contrast between foreground and background. **Figure 17.1** shows the best combination to use for readability: black text on a white background.

In order to make text readable make sure that you have enough contrast between the text and the background.	White text on a black background is hard to read
In order to make text readable make sure that you have enough contrast between the text and the background.	Make sure you have enough contrast between the text and the background
In order to make text readable make sure that you have enough contrast between the text and the background.	The best combination for readability is black text on a white background

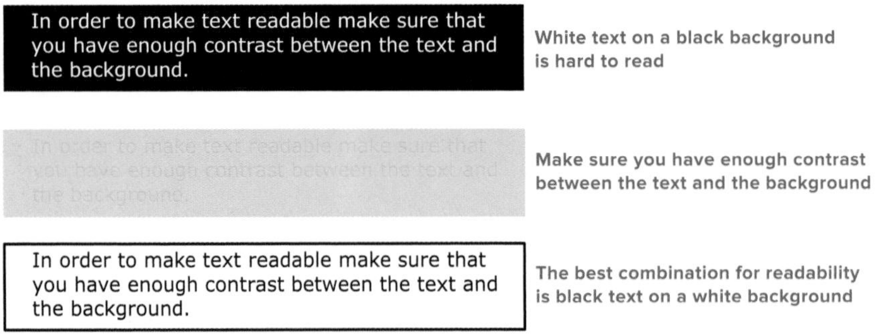

FIGURE 17.1 Black text on a white background is easiest to read

Takeaways

✳ Use a large point size for text that will be read on a computer screen. This will help to minimize eye strain.

✳ Break text up into chunks. Use bullets, short paragraphs, and pictures.

✳ Provide ample contrast between foreground and background. Black text on a white background is the most readable.

✳ Make sure your content is worth reading. In the end, it all boils down to whether or not the text on the page is of interest to your audience.

18 PEOPLE READ FASTER WITH A LONGER LINE LENGTH, BUT THEY PREFER A SHORTER LINE LENGTH

Have you ever had to decide what column width to use on a screen? Should it be a wide column with 100 characters per line? Or a short column with 50 characters per line? Or something in between? The answer depends on whether you want people to read faster or to like the page.

Mary Dyson (2004) conducted research on line length, and combed other studies to determine what line length people prefer. Her work showed that 100 characters per line is the optimal length for on-screen reading *speed*; but we *prefer* a short or medium line length (45 to 72 characters per line). **Figure 18.1** shows examples of a short and long line length.

People read faster with a longer line length.

We prefer a short line length

FIGURE 18.1 Line length, speed, and preference, www.maderalabs.com

Every time you get to the end of a line, you interrupt saccade and fixation eye movement. A shorter line length creates more of these interruptions over the total length of the piece you are reading.

The research also found that we can read a single wide column faster than multiple columns, but we prefer multiple columns, like those shown in **Figure 18.2**.

BUCKS
Be Cynical About the Refinance Process

BY JENNIFER SARANOW SCHULTZ
DECEMBER 17, 2010

As least until recently, we've been in the midst of a refinancing boom. So consumers applying for refinancings should at least expect some delays.

While lenders are leery about releasing details about how long refinancings are taking to close today versus a year ago, some are willing to admit that processing

being enforced and regulatory changes enacted" to ensure that consumers can safely afford their mortgages. She also pointed to the low rates.

"While Bank of America is proud to be playing a leading role in this new era of responsible lending, we also understand that these changes often translate into longer processing periods," Ms. Yamamoto said. "This is the reality across the industry."

sideration of the environment, we currently are locking refinance interest rates for a period of 90 days." In addition, she said, if it is necessary to extend the closing period beyond 90 days and "it is determined that the delay is on the bank's side, we will extend the rate lock at no cost to our customer." She noted that Bank of America is also working to increase its "mortgage fulfillment capacity."

Chase, meanwhile, offers customers

FIGURE 18.2 People read faster with one single-wide column, but they prefer multiple columns

If you ask people which they prefer, they will say multiple columns with short line lengths. Interestingly, if you ask them which they read faster, they will insist it is also the multiple columns with short line lengths, even though the data shows otherwise.

Takeaways

＊ Line length presents a quandary: Do you give people the short line length and multiple columns that they prefer, or go against their own preference and intuition, knowing that they will read faster if you use a longer line length and a single column?

＊ Use a longer line length (100 characters per line) if reading speed is an issue.

＊ Use a shorter line length (45 to 72 characters per line) if reading speed is less critical.

＊ For a multipage article, consider using multiple columns and a short line length (45 characters per line).

HOW PEOPLE REMEMBER

Let's start with a memory test. Read over the following list of terms for about 30 seconds, and then keep reading the chapter:

Meeting	**Computer**	**Phone**
Work	**Papers**	**Chair**
Presentation	**Pen**	**Shelf**
Office	**Staff**	**Table**
Deadline	**Whiteboard**	**Secretary**

We'll come back to this list later. First, let's learn about the frailties and complexities of human memory.

19 SHORT-TERM MEMORY IS LIMITED

We've all experienced this moment: you're on the phone and the person you're talking to gives you the name and number of someone you need to call right away. You don't have a pen or paper to write down the information, so you repeat the name and number over and over to help yourself remember them. You try to get off the phone quickly so you can make the call while the number is still running through your head. You may find that your memory isn't very reliable in this situation.

Psychologists have many theories about how this type of memory works: some refer to it as short-term memory, others as working memory. In this chapter we'll call this type of quick memory—the memory you need for less than a minute—*working memory*.

WORKING MEMORY AND FOCUSED ATTENTION

There's only so much people can hold in working memory before they forget it. Information in working memory is easily interfered with. For example, if you're trying to remember a name and phone number, and someone starts talking to you at the same time, you're probably going to get very annoyed. You're also going to forget the name and number. If you don't concentrate, you'll lose it from working memory. This is because working memory is tied to your ability to focus attention. To maintain information in working memory, you must keep your attention focused on it.

 The brain lights up when working memory is active

Theories about memory date to the 1800s. Now researchers can use fMRI technology to actually *see* which parts of the brain are active when people perform various tasks and engage with different images, words, and sounds. When a task involves working memory, the prefrontal cortex (which focuses attention) lights up. Other parts of the brain are also active during tasks that employ working memory. For example, if the task includes remembering words or numbers, then there will also be activity in the left hemisphere. If the task involves spatial relations, such as finding something on a map, then the right hemisphere will also be active.

Perhaps the most interesting finding is that the connection between these areas of the brain and the prefrontal cortex increases when working memory is in use. While working memory is active, the prefrontal cortex is choosing strategies and deciding what to pay attention to; this has a significant impact on memory.

Scans of the brain using functional magnetic resonance imaging (fMRI) show that there is less activity in the prefrontal cortex (the part of your brain right behind your forehead) when you're under stress. This indicates that stress reduces the effectiveness of working memory.

WORKING MEMORY VS. SENSORY INPUT

Interestingly, there is an inverse relationship between working memory and the amount of sensory input you're processing at any given time. People with high-functioning working memories are better able to screen out what's going on around them. Your prefrontal cortex determines what you should pay attention to. If you can tune out all the sensory stimuli around you, and instead focus your attention on the one thing in your working memory, you'll be able to remember it.

 More working memory equals better performance in school

Recent research links working memory and academic success. Tracy Alloway (2010) tested the working memory capacity of a group of five-year-olds, and then tracked the children over time. Working memory at age five predicted how well the children did through high school and beyond: those with higher working memory capacities were more successful academically. This shouldn't be a surprise, since working memory is involved in remembering instructions from a teacher, and, as we will discuss later, is part of long-term memory. What is interesting, though, is that working memory can be tested; then, if the child's score is low, the results can be used to plan an intervention. It's a relatively fast and easy way to find out which students are at risk for school problems, and it gives educators and parents the opportunity to tackle those problems early on.

Takeaways

✻ Don't ask people to remember information from one place to another, such as reading letters or numbers on one page and then entering them on another page; if you do, they'll probably forget the information and get frustrated.

✻ If you ask people to remember things in working memory, don't ask them to do anything else until they've completed that task. Working memory is sensitive to interference—too much sensory input will prevent them from focusing attention.

20 PEOPLE REMEMBER ONLY FOUR ITEMS AT ONCE

If you're familiar with usability, psychology, or memory research, you've probably heard the phrase "the magical number seven, plus or minus two." This refers, actually, to what I would call an urban legend: George A. Miller (1956) wrote a research paper showing that people can remember from five to nine (seven plus or minus two) things, and that people can process seven plus or minus two pieces of information at a time. So you should only put five to nine items on a menu, or have five to nine tabs on a screen. Have you heard that story? Well, it's not quite accurate.

WHY IT'S AN URBAN LEGEND

Psychologist Alan Baddeley questioned the seven plus or minus two rule. Baddeley (1994) dug up Miller's paper and discovered that it wasn't a paper describing actual research; it was a talk that Miller gave at a professional meeting. And it was basically Miller thinking out loud about whether there is some kind of inherent limit to the amount of information that people can process at a time.

Baddeley (1986) conducted a long series of studies on human memory and information processing. Others, including Nelson Cowan (2001), followed in his footsteps. The research now shows that the "magical" number is four.

USING CHUNKS TO TURN FOUR INTO MORE

People can hold three or four things in working memory as long as they aren't distracted and their processing of the information is not interfered with.

One of the interesting strategies people employ to help our fragile memories is "chunking" information together into groups. It's no accident that U.S. phone numbers look like this:

712-569-4532

Instead of having to remember 10 separate numerals, a phone number has three chunks, with four or less items in each chunk. If you know the area code by heart (that is, it's stored in long-term memory), then you don't have to remember that part of the number, so you can ignore one whole chunk.

Years ago phone numbers were easier to remember because you mainly called people in your area code, so you didn't have to hold the area code in working memory. It was in long-term memory, which we will get to shortly. In the good old days you didn't even need to use the area code if the number you were calling from was in the same area code as you were dialing from (not true anymore in most places). And to make it even easier, everyone in town had the same exchange (the 569 part of the previous phone number). If you were dialing someone in your town with the same exchange, all you had to remember was the last four numbers. No problem! (I know I'm dating myself here by telling you how it used to be back in the old days. I live now in a small town in Wisconsin, and people here still give their number to others as the last four digits only, even though just four numbers won't work anymore).

THE FOUR-ITEM RULE APPLIES TO MEMORY RETRIEVAL, TOO

The four-item rule applies not only to working memory, but also to long-term memory. George Mandler (1969) showed that people could memorize information in categories and then retrieve it from memory perfectly if there were one to three items in a category. The number of items recalled dropped steadily when each category contained more than three items. If there were four to six items in a category, then people could remember 80 percent of the items. It went down from there, falling to 20 percent if there were 80 items in the category (**Figure 20.1**).

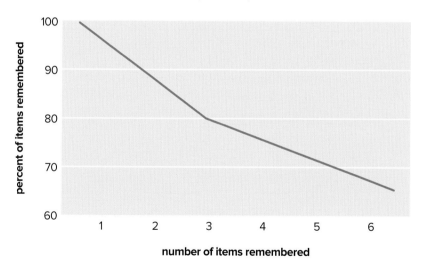

FIGURE 20.1 The more people are asked to recall, the less accurate their recollection is

Donald Broadbent (1975) asked people to recall items in different categories, for example, the Seven Dwarfs, the seven colors of the rainbow, the countries of Europe, or the names of current shows on TV. People remembered two, three, or four items clustered together.

⭐ Even chimps can do it

Nobuyuki Kawai and Tetsuro Matsuzawa (2000) trained a chimpanzee to take memory tests similar to the ones that are given to humans. The chimpanzee (named Ai) could correctly complete the memory tasks with 95 percent accuracy when she had to memorize four numbers. She was only 65 percent correct when there were five numbers.

Takeaways

＊ If you could limit the information you give people to four items, that would actually be a great idea, but you don't have to be that drastic. You can use more pieces of information as long as you group and chunk.

＊ Include no more than four items in each chunk.

＊ Be aware that people tend to use external aids (notes, lists, calendars, appointment books) so they don't have to rely on memory.

21 PEOPLE HAVE TO USE INFORMATION TO MAKE IT STICK

How do people move things from working memory into long-term memory? There are basically two ways: repeat it a lot, or connect it to something they already know.

REPETITION PHYSICALLY CHANGES THE BRAIN

There are 10 billion neurons in the brain that store information. Electrical impulses flow through a neuron and are moved by neuron-transmitting chemicals across the synaptic gap between neurons. Neurons in the brain fire every time we repeat a word, phrase, song, or phone number we are trying to memorize. Memories are stored as patterns of connections between neurons. When two neurons are activated, the connections between them are strengthened.

If we repeat the information enough times, the neurons form a firing trace. Once the trace is formed, then just starting the sequence triggers the rest of the items, and allows us to retrieve the memory. This is why we need to hear information over and over to make it stick.

Experience causes physical changes in our brain. In a few seconds new circuits are formed that can forever change the way we think about something or remember information.

THE POWER OF A SCHEMA

If I ask you to describe what a "head" is, you might talk about the brain, hair, eyes, nose, ears, skin, neck, and other parts. A head is made up of many things, but you've gathered all that information together and called it "head." Similarly I could talk about the "eye." You would think about all the things that make up an eye: the eyeball, iris, eyelash, eyelid, and so on. The head is a schema. The eye is a schema. People use schemata (plural for schema) to store information in long-term memory and to retrieve it.

If people can connect new information to information that is already stored, then it's easier to make it stick, or stay in long-term memory, and easier to retrieve it. Schemata

FIGURE 21.1 A head is made up of eyes, ears, nose, mouth, hair, and other parts. Combining those parts into one schema makes them easier to remember.

allow people to build up these associations in long-term memory. Just one schema helps them organize a lot of information (**Figure 21.1**).

EXPERTS STORE INFORMATION AS SCHEMATA

The better people are at something, the more organized and powerful their schema about it will be. For example, players who are new to the game of chess need a lot of little schemata: the first schema might be how to set up the pieces on the board, the second might be how a queen can move, and so on. But expert chess players can pile a lot of information into one schema with ease. They can look at a chessboard in the middle of a game and tell you what some of the starting moves were, the strategies for each player, and what the next move is likely to be. They could certainly recite how to set up the board and how each piece can move. What would take many schemata for novice players, expert players can store in one schema. This makes retrieval of information faster and easier, and makes it easier for the expert to put new information about chess into long-term memory. The expert can remember a lot of information as a single chunk (**Figure 21.2**).

FIGURE 21.2 For experts, everything on the chessboard is in one schema

---

Takeaways

＊ If you want people to remember something, then you have to go over it again and again. Practice really does make perfect.

＊ One of the major reasons to do user or customer research is so that you can identify and understand the schemata that your particular target audience has.

＊ If people already have a schema that relates to information that you are providing, make sure you point out what that schema is. It will be easier for them to learn and remember the information if they can plug it into an existing schema.

22 IT'S EASIER TO RECOGNIZE INFORMATION THAN RECALL IT

Remember the memory test at the start of this chapter? Without looking at the list, write down as many of the words as you can. We'll use this memory test to talk about recognition and recall.

RECOGNITION IS EASIER THAN RECALL

In the memory test you just took, you memorized a list of words, and later wrote them down. This is called a *recall task.* If instead I had shown you a list of words, or even walked you into the office and asked you which items were on the list, I would have been giving you a *recognition task.* Recognition is easier than recall. Recognition makes use of context. And context can help you remember.

INCLUSION ERRORS

All the words you memorized were things related to an office. Look at what you wrote down, and compare your list with the original list at the beginning of the chapter. You probably wrote words that weren't even in the original list, but that go with the "office" schema. For example, you might have written down "desk" or "pencil" or "boss." Consciously or unconsciously, you were aware that the list included things associated with an office. The schema probably helped you remember items on the list, but it might also have caused you to make errors of inclusion.

 Children make fewer inclusion errors

When children under age five are shown items or pictures and then asked what they remember, they actually make fewer errors of inclusion than adults because their schemata are not as well formed.

Takeaways

✳ Eliminate memory load whenever possible. Many user interface design guidelines and interface features have evolved over the years to mitigate issues with human memory.

✳ Try not to require people to recall information. It's much easier for them to recognize information than recall it from memory.

23 MEMORY TAKES A LOT OF MENTAL RESOURCES

The latest research on unconscious mental processing shows that people receive 40 billion sensory inputs every second, and are consciously aware of 40 at any one time. Doesn't this mean that we can deal with and remember more than four things at a time? When you perceive a sensory input (for example, a sound, the feel of the wind on your skin, a rock that is in front of you), you perceive that something exists. You don't have to remember it necessarily or do something with the information. Conscious awareness of 40 things is different than consciously processing 40 bits of information. It takes a lot of mental resources to think about, remember, process, represent, and encode information.

MEMORY IS EASILY DISRUPTED

Imagine you're listening to a presentation at a conference. When the presentation is finished, you meet your friend in the lobby of the hotel. "What was the talk about?" she asks. You're most likely to remember what was seen and heard at the end of the talk. This is called the *recency effect*.

If your phone vibrates during a presentation and you stop listening for a minute to text someone, then you are most likely to remember the beginning of the presentation and forget the ending. This is called the *suffix effect*.

Interesting facts about memory

★ You can store concrete words (table, chair) in long-term memory more easily than abstract words (justice, democracy).

★ When you're sad you tend to remember sad things.

★ You can't remember much before the age of three.

★ You can remember things that you see (visual memory) better than words.

People sleep and dream so we will remember

Some of the best research happens through serendipity. In 1991 Neuroscientist Matthew Wilson. was studying brain activity in rats as they ran mazes. One day he accidentally left the rats hooked up to the equipment he used to record their brain activity. The rats eventually fell asleep. To his surprise he found that their brain activity was almost the same whether they were sleeping or running mazes.

Daoyun Ji and Wilson (2007) started a series of experiments to study this further. Their experiments have led them to a theory, not just about rats, but about people, too: when people sleep and dream, they are reworking, or consolidating, their experiences from the day. Specifically, they are consolidating new memories and making new associations from the information they processed during the day. Their brains are deciding what to remember and what to forget.

 ## Why rhymes are easier to remember

Phonological (sound of words) coding can help retrieve information. Before there was written language, stories were memorized and retold in rhyming verse. The activation of one line in a verse more easily triggers the next verse. For example, you may have learned, "Thirty days hath September, April, June, and November." This is an example of phonological coding.

Takeaways

✳ Use concrete terms and icons. They will be easier to remember.

✳ Let people rest (and even sleep) if you want them to remember information.

✳ Try not to interrupt people if they are learning or encoding information.

✳ Information in the middle of a presentation will be the least likely to be remembered.

24 PEOPLE RECONSTRUCT MEMORIES EACH TIME THEY REMEMBER THEM

Think back to a particular event that happened at least five years ago. Maybe it was a wedding, a family gathering, a dinner with friends, or a vacation. Remember the people, and where you were. Maybe you can remember the weather, or what you were wearing.

MEMORIES CHANGE

When you think about this event, it probably plays in your mind like a short movie clip. Because you experience memories this way, you tend to think that memories are stored in their entirety and never change, like an archived movie. But that's not what happens.

Memories are actually reconstructed every time we think of them. They're not movie clips that are stored in the brain in a certain location, like files on a hard drive. They are nerve pathways that fire anew each time we remember the event. This makes for some interesting effects. For example, the memory can change each time it is retrieved.

Other events that occur after the original event can change the memory of the original event. At the original event, you and your cousin were close friends. But later on you have an argument and a falling-out that lasts for years. Over time when you recall the memory of the first event, it changes without you realizing it. It starts to include your cousin being aloof and cold, even if that is not true. The later experience has changed your memory.

You'll also start to fill in memory gaps with made-up sequences of events, but these will seem as real to you as the original event. You can't remember who else was at the family dinner, but Aunt Jolene is usually present at these events, and so over time your memory of the event will include Aunt Jolene, even if she wasn't there.

WHY EYEWITNESS TESTIMONIES ARE UNRELIABLE

In her research on reconstructive memory, Elizabeth Loftus (1974) would show participants a video clip of an automobile accident. Then she would ask a series of questions about the accident, and substitute critical words. For example, she might ask, "How fast would you estimate the car was going when it hit the other vehicle?" or "How fast would you estimate the car was going when it smashed the other vehicle?" And she would ask the participants if they remembered seeing broken glass.

Notice the difference in using the word "hit" versus "smashed." When Loftus used the word "smashed," the estimated speed was higher than when she used the word "hit." And more than twice as many people remembered seeing broken glass if the word "smashed" was used rather than the word "hit." In later research Loftus and Palmer were even able to inject memories of events that never happened.

 Have witnesses close their eyes

If witnesses close their eyes while trying to remember what they saw, their memories are clearer and more accurate (Perfect, 2008).

 Memories can, indeed, be erased

Did you see *Eternal Sunshine of the Spotless Mind?* It's a movie about a business that erases particular memories. It turns out that is possible. Research by scientists at Johns Hopkins (Roger Clem, 2010) shows that memories can actually be erased.

Takeaways

✳ If you're testing or interviewing customers about a product, the words you use can affect greatly what people "remember."

✳ Don't rely on self-reports of past behavior. People will not remember accurately what they or others did or said.

✳ Take what people say after the fact—when they are remembering using your product, for instance, or remembering the experience of calling your customer service line— with a grain of salt.

25 IT'S A GOOD THING THAT PEOPLE FORGET

Forgetting things seems to be such a problem. At best it's annoying ("Where did I put my keys?"), and at worst it can send the wrong people to prison with inaccurate eyewitness testimonies. How could something so maladaptive have developed in humans? Why are we so flawed?

It's actually not a flaw. Think about all the sensory inputs and experiences you have every minute, every day, every year, and throughout your lifetime. If you remembered every single thing, you'd be unable to function; you have to forget some things. Your brain is constantly deciding what to remember and what to forget. It doesn't always make decisions that you find helpful, but in general, the decisions it makes (primarily unconsciously) are keeping you alive!

A FORMULA TO SHOW YOU HOW MUCH YOU WILL FORGET

In 1886, Hermann Ebbinghaus created a formula showing the degradation of memories:

$$R = e^{(-t/S)}$$

Where R is memory retention, S is the relative strength of memory, and t is time.

The formula results in a graph that looks like **Figure 25.1**. It's called the Forgetting Curve, and it shows that we quickly forget information unless it's stored in long-term memory.

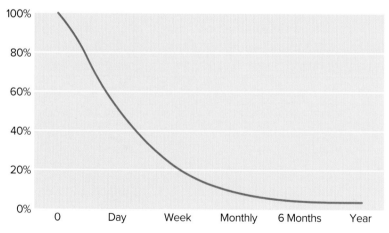

FIGURE 25.1 Hermann Ebbinghaus's Forgetting Curve

* People are always going to forget.

* What people forget is not a conscious decision.

* Design with forgetting in mind. If some information is really important, don't rely on people to remember it. Provide it for them in your design, or have a way for them to easily look it up.

26 THE MOST VIVID MEMORIES ARE WRONG

If I asked you to recall where you were and what you were doing when you first heard about the September 11, 2001, attacks in New York City, chances are very good that you could tell me about that day in great detail. If you live in the U.S., and you were age ten or older on that date, your memory would likely include details such as how you heard about the attacks, who you were with, and what you did the rest of that day. But research shows that a lot of, perhaps even most of, your memories would be wrong.

FLASHBULB MEMORIES ARE VIVID

Remembering traumatic or dramatic events in great detail is called "flashbulb memory." Emotions are processed in the amygdala, which is very close to the hippocampus, which is involved in the long-term coding of information into memories. So it's no surprise to psychologists that emotionally laden memories might be very strong and remembered vividly.

VIVID BUT FULL OF ERRORS

Although flashbulb memories are vivid, they are also full of errors. In 1986 the space shuttle *Challenger* exploded. If you to recall that event, you probably remember it vividly. The day after this tragic event, Ulric Neisser, a professor who researches memories like these, he had his students write down their memories of what had happened. Three years later he asked them to write their memory of the event again (Neisser, 1992). Over 90 percent of the later reports differed from the originals. Half of them were inaccurate in two-thirds of the details. One person, when shown the description she had written three years earlier, said, "I know that's my handwriting, but I couldn't possibly have written that." Similar research has been conducted on individuals with memories of the 9/11 attacks, with similar results.

The Ebbinghaus Forgetting Curve showed that memories degrade quickly over time. Because flashbulb memories are so vivid, it was thought that perhaps they were not as subject to forgetting as other memories. But it turns out they are. That's kind of disturbing when you think about it. Because these memories are so vivid, we tend to think they are more true. But we are wrong.

Takeaways

✳ If you know that someone had a dramatic or traumatic experience, you need to understand two things: 1. They'll be convinced that what they remember is true and 2. It isn't exactly true!

HOW
PEOPLE
THINK

The brain has 23 billion neurons. That's a lot of capacity for mental processing. So what's going on in there?

Understanding how people think is crucial if you're going to design for them. Just as there are visual illusions, there are also thinking illusions. This chapter describes some of the interesting things the brain does as it makes sense of the world.

27 PEOPLE PROCESS INFORMATION BETTER IN BITE-SIZED CHUNKS

The brain can only process small amount of information at a time—consciously, that is. (The estimate is that you handle 40 billion pieces of information every second, but only 40 of those make it to your conscious brain.) One mistake that designers sometimes make is giving too much information all at once.

APPLYING THE CONCEPT OF PROGRESSIVE DISCLOSURE

Progressive disclosure means providing only the information people need at the moment.

The figures below show an example of progressive disclosure from MailChimp (from www.mailchimp.com. MailChimp is a trademark of The Rocket Science Group, LLC). Rather than putting a full description of what you can do with the service on the first page, there is just a list and an image for each activity (**Figure 27.1**). When people click on one of the activities, they get a little more information (**Figure 27.2**), and then they can go a level further for more details (**Figure 27.3**). By giving them a little information at a time, you avoid overwhelming them, and also address the needs of different people—some may want a high-level overview, whereas others are looking for all the detail.

FIGURE 27.1 The first step in progressive disclosure

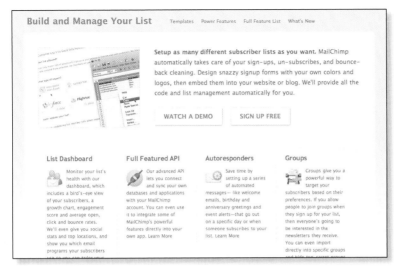

FIGURE 27.2 The second step gives a little more detail

FIGURE 27.3 The last step is for people who want even more information

COUNTING CLICKS ISN'T WHAT COUNTS

Progressive disclosure requires multiple clicks. You may have heard it said that Web sites should minimize the number of times that people have to click to get to detailed information. The number of clicks is not important. People are very willing to click multiple times. In fact, they won't even notice they're clicking if they're getting the right amount of information at each click to keep them going down the path. Think progressive disclosure; don't count clicks.

KNOW WHO NEEDS WHAT WHEN

Progressive disclosure is a great technique, but it assumes that you know what most people want most of the time. If you haven't done your research on that, then you could end up with a frustrating site, with most people having to spend a lot of time searching for the information they are looking for. Progressive disclosure only works if you know what most people will be looking for at each part of the path.

 Read Krug for more information

A great book about designing interfaces that don't require people to think too much is Steve Krug's *Don't Make Me Think.*

 The origins of progressive disclosure

The term progressive disclosure was first used by J.M. Keller. Keller is a professor of instructional design, and in the early 1980s he came up with an instructional design model called Attention, Relevance, Confidence, and Satisfaction (ARCS). Progressive disclosure is part of the ARCS model: present only the information the learner needs at that moment.

Takeaways

＊ Use progressive disclosure. Show people what they need when they need it. Build in links for them to get more information.

＊ If you have to make a trade-off on clicks versus thinking, use more clicks and less thinking.

＊ Before you use progressive disclosure, make sure you've done your research and know what most people want and when they want it.

28 SOME TYPES OF MENTAL PROCESSING ARE MORE CHALLENGING THAN OTHERS

Imagine you're paying bills at your online banking Web site. You have to think about what bills need to be paid when, look up your balance, decide how much to pay on your credit cards, and click the right buttons to get the payments processed. As you do this task, there are things you're thinking about and remembering (cognitive), things you're looking at on the screen (visual), and buttons you are pressing, mouse movements, and typing (motor).

In human factors terminology, these are called *loads*. The theory is that there are basically three different kinds of demands or loads that you can make on a person: cognitive (including memory), visual, and motor.

ALL LOADS ARE NOT EQUAL

Each load uses up a different amount of mental resources. You use up more resources when you ask people to look at something or find something on a screen (visual) than when you ask them to press a button or move a mouse (motor). You use up more by asking them to think or remember or do a mental calculation (cognitive), than when you ask them to look at something on a screen (visual). So from a human factors point of view, the order of the loads from most "expensive" to least is:

★ Cognitive

★ Visual

★ Motor

MAKING TRADE-OFFS

From a human factors point of view, when you're designing a product, application, or Web site, you're always making trade-offs. If you have to add a few clicks, but it means that the person doesn't have to think or remember as much, that's worth it, because adding clicks is less of a load than thinking. I once did some research on this topic. People had to go through more than 10 clicks to get the task done, and at the end they would look up and smile and say, "That was easy!" because each step was logical and gave them what they expected. They didn't have to think. Clicking is less of a load than thinking.

USE FITT'S LAW TO DETERMINE MOTOR LOADS

Although motor loads are the least "expensive" of the three loads, you often want to reduce them. One way to reduce the motor load is to make sure that the targets you're asking people to hit aren't too small or too far away, for example, when you ask them to move a mouse across a screen and click a button or a small arrow on a drop-down box to show a list of choices.

There is actually a formula that can be used to figure out how large a target should be to enable someone to reach it reliably while moving a mouse across the screen. It's called Fitt's Law. The formula is shown in **Figure 28.1**.

$$T = a + b \log_2\left(1 + \frac{D}{W}\right)$$

FIGURE 28.1 The formula for Fitt's Law

★ T is the average time taken to complete the movement (sometimes called MT for Movement Time).

★ a is the start/stop time of the device (intercept) and b stands for the inherent speed of the device (slope).

★ D is the distance from the starting point to the center of the target.

★ W is the width of the target measured along the axis of motion.

I don't expect you to go calculate Fitt's Law, but I include it here so that you realize that there is a scientific way to determine how large a button or arrow should be.

The basic idea to keep in mind is that there is a relationship between speed, accuracy, and distance. For example, let's say that you have a small arrow on the bottom right of the screen and the user has to move the mouse from the top left to the bottom right to click the small arrow. Fitt's Law tells us that they will probably overshoot the arrow if they move quickly, and they'll have to back up and go to the arrow.

 Minimize motor switching

One type of motor load is when people have to switch back and forth between a keyboard and a mouse or trackpad. This is especially true of people who are doing "heads down" data entry. If someone is typing or entering data from paper, and they do it a lot and are very skilled, chances are they are not looking at anything but the paper (hence the term "heads down"). In this case it can be distracting to move from keyboard to mouse. If possible, keep people on the keyboard or with the mouse as long as possible and minimize the switching.

SOMETIMES YOU WANT TO INCREASE LOADS

Most of the time when we consider loads in design, we're looking to reduce the loads (especially cognitive and visual) to make the product easier to use. But sometimes you want to increase the load. For example, to grab someone's attention you might add visual information (pictures, animation, video) and thereby increase the visual load of the product.

The best example of purposely increasing loads is gaming. A game is an interface where one or more of the loads have been intentionally increased to provide challenge. Some games have high cognitive loads because you have to figure out what's going on. Some have high visual loads, where you have to find things on the screen. Some have high motor loads, where you have to use the keyboard or a separate device to move the cursor, or "shoot" the villains. Many games increase more than one load, for example, if the game has both visual and motor challenges.

Takeaways

✳ Evaluate the loads of an existing product to see if you should reduce one or more of the loads to make it easier to use.

✳ When you design a product, remember that making people think or remember (cognitive load) requires the most mental resources.

✳ Look for trade-offs, for example, where you can reduce a cognitive load by increasing a visual or motor load.

✳ Make sure your targets are large enough to be easily reached.

29 MINDS WANDER 30 PERCENT OF THE TIME

You're at work reading a report that a colleague has written and you realize that you've just read the same sentence about three times. Instead of thinking about what you were reading, your mind wandered.

Mind wandering is similar to but not the same as daydreaming. Psychologists use *daydreaming* to refer to any stray thoughts, fantasies, or stories you imagine, for example, winning the lottery or being a celebrity. *Mind wandering* is more specific: it refers to doing one task and then fading into thinking about something unrelated to that task.

MIND WANDERING IS A VERY COMMON PHENOMENON

People underestimate mind wandering; according to Jonathan Schooler of the University of California, Santa Barbara, people think their minds are wandering about 10 percent of the time, when it's actually much more than that. During everyday activities your minds wander up to 30 percent of the time, and in some cases, such as driving on an uncrowded highway, it might be as high as 70 percent.

 Wandering minds annoy neuroscientists

Some neuroscientists became interested in studying wandering minds because they were such an annoyance while doing brain scan research (Mason, 2007). The researchers would have subjects perform a certain task (for example, look at a picture or read a passage) while scanning for brain activity. About 30 percent of the time there would be extraneous results that seemed unrelated to the task at hand. That's because the subject's mind was wandering from the task at hand. Eventually researchers decided to start studying the wandering mind rather than just get annoyed by it.

WHY A WANDERING MIND CAN BE A GOOD THING

Mind wandering allows one part of the brain to focus on the task at hand, and another part of the brain to keep a higher goal in mind. For example, while driving you're paying attention to the road, but you're also thinking about when to stop for gas. Or you are reading an article online about a cholesterol medication that your doctor thinks you should take, but your mind wanders to the idea that you should put that appointment with the hair salon on your calendar. Mind wandering might be the closest thing we have to multitasking. It's not really multitasking (which doesn't exist—see the "How People Focus Their Attention" chapter for more information), but mind wandering does allow you to switch focus from one idea to another, and then back again quickly.

WHY A WANDERING MIND CAN BE A BAD THING

Much of the time when your mind wanders, you're unaware of it. More "zoning out" than mind wandering, this means that you can miss important information. For example, if you are supposed to be reading that report from your colleague, but you are instead thinking about what to make for dinner, that may just mean you are being unproductive. You aren't usually aware when you're zoning out.

 More mind wandering equals more creativity

Researchers at the University of California, Santa Barbara (Christoff, 2009) have evidence that people whose minds wander a lot are more creative and better problem solvers. Their brains have them working on the task at hand, but are simultaneously processing other information and making connections.

Takeaways

＊ People will only focus on a task for a limited time. Assume that their minds are wandering often.

＊ If possible, use hyperlinks to grab onto this idea of quickly switching from topic to topic. People like Web surfing because it enables this type of wandering.

＊ Make sure you build in feedback about where people are so that if they wander, it's easier for them to get back to the original location or go to the next.

30 THE MORE UNCERTAIN PEOPLE ARE, THE MORE THEY DEFEND THEIR IDEAS

I'm a staunch Apple convert. I wasn't always an Apple fan; I used to be a Windows/PC person. Realize that I go all the way back to when PCs first came out. I used to have a marvelous "portable" PC that ran on a CPM operating system and had two (count 'em, *two*) 360 KB (yes, I said KB) floppy disk drives (in other words, *no* hard drive). I was a PC person, *not* an Apple person. Apples were for teachers and then later, for artsy people. That was not me.

Fast forward to today and I will be talking on my iPhone, while charging my iPod for my afternoon exercise, while transferring a movie to my iPad from my MacBook Pro, which I might decide to watch on my television via Apple TV. What the heck happened here? (I describe the story of how I changed my loyalty from PCs to Apple in my book *Neuro Web Design: What Makes Them Click?* It's a matter of starting with small changes and commitments and then growing to more loyalty).

So you might be able to guess what happened when I went to dinner with a colleague who was showing me his Android phone. He loves his new Android phone and wanted to show me all the ways it was as good as, or better than, my iPhone. I was totally uninterested in hearing about it. I didn't even want to look at it. Basically, I didn't want to allow into my brain any information that would conflict with my opinion that anything besides an iPhone was even a possibility. I was showing classical symptoms of *cognitive dissonance denial.*

ALTER OUR BELIEFS OR DENY THE INFORMATION?

In 1956 Leon Festinger wrote a book called *When Prophecy Fails.* In it he describes the idea of cognitive dissonance. Cognitive dissonance is the uncomfortable feeling you get when you have two ideas that conflict with each other. You don't like the feeling, so you'll try to get rid of the dissonance. There are two main ways you can do that: change your belief, or deny one of the ideas.

When forced, people will change their beliefs

In the original research on cognitive dissonance, people were forced to defend an opinion that they did not believe in. The result was that people tended to change their beliefs to fit the new idea.

In new research by Vincent Van Veen (2009) had people "argue" that the fMRI scan experience was pleasant (it's not). When "forced" to make statements that the experience was pleasant, certain parts of the brain lit up (the dorsal anterior cingulate cortex and the anterior insular cortex). The more these regions were activated, the more the participant would claim that he really did think the fMRI was pleasant.

When not forced, people dig in

There's another reaction that sometimes occurs. What if you are not forced to state that you believe something you don't; what if instead you are presented with information that opposes your beliefs, but you are not forced to espouse a new belief. In these situations the tendency is to deny the new information instead of changing your belief to fit.

If uncertain, people will argue harder

David Gal and Derek Rucker (2010) recently conducted research where they used framing techniques to make people feel uncertain. (For example, they told one group to remember a time when they were full of certainty, and the other group to remember a time when they were full of doubt.) Then they asked the participants whether they were meat-eaters, vegetarians, vegans, or otherwise, how important this was to them, and how confident they were in their opinions. People who were asked to remember a time of uncertainty were less confident of their eating choices. However, when asked to write up their beliefs to persuade someone else to eat the way they did, they would write more and stronger arguments than those who were certain of their choice. Gal and Rucker performed the research with different topics (for example, preferences for a Mac versus a PC computer) and found similar results. When people were less certain, they would dig in and argue even harder.

Takeaways

* Don't spend a lot of time trying to change someone's ingrained beliefs.

* The best way to change a belief is to get someone to commit to something very small.

* Don't just give people evidence that their belief is not logical, or tenable, or a good choice. This may backfire and make them dig in even harder.

31 PEOPLE CREATE MENTAL MODELS

Imagine that you've never seen an iPad, but I've just handed you one and told you that you can read books on it. Before you turn on the iPad, before you use it, you have a model in your head of what reading a book on the iPad will be like. You have assumptions about what the book will look like on the screen, what things you will be able to do, and how you will do them—things like turning a page, or using a book-mark. You have a *mental model* of reading a book on the iPad, even if you've never done it before.

What that mental model in your head looks and acts like depends on many things. If you've used an iPad before, your mental model of reading a book on an iPad will be different than that of someone who has never used one, or who doesn't even know what an iPad is. If you've been using a Kindle for the past year, then your mental model will be different from someone who has never read a book electronically. And once you get the iPad and read a couple books on it, whichever mental model you had in your head before will start to change and adjust to reflect your experience.

I've been talking about mental models (and their counterparts, conceptual models, discussed below) since the 1980s. I've been designing interfaces for software, Web sites, medical devices, and various products for many years. I always enjoy the challenge of matching what's going on in people's brains with the constraints and opportunities presented by technology. Interface environments come and go (for example, the green screen of character-based systems, or the blue screen of early graphical user interfaces), but people change more slowly. Some of the age-old user interface design concepts are still extremely relevant and important. Mental models and conceptual models are some of the most useful design concepts that I believe have passed the test of time.

 The origin of the term *mental models*

The first person to talk about mental models was Kenneth Craik in his 1943 book, *The Nature of Explanation.* Shortly thereafter, Craik died in a bicycle accident and the concept went dormant for many years. It reappeared in the 1980s, when two books were published with the title *Mental Models,* one by Philip Johnson-Laird and the other by Dedre Gentner.

The best history I've found about mental models as they relate to software and usability is a 1999 article by Mary Jo Davidson, Laura Dove, and Julie Weltz called "Mental Models and Usability." (http://www.lauradove.info/reports/mental%20models.htm)

WHAT EXACTLY IS A MENTAL MODEL?

There are many definitions for mental models that have been around for at least 25 years. One of my favorites is from Susan Carey's 1986 journal article "Cognitive Science and Science Education," which states:

"A mental model represents a person's thought process for how something works (i.e., a person's understanding of the surrounding world). Mental models are based on incomplete facts, past experiences, and even intuitive perceptions. They help shape actions and behavior, influence what people pay attention to in complicated situations, and define how people approach and solve problems."

WHAT IS A MENTAL MODEL IN DESIGN?

In the field of design, a mental model refers to the representation of something—the real world, a device, software, and so on—that a person has in mind. People create mental models very quickly, often before they even use the software or device. Their mental models come from their prior experience with similar software or devices, assumptions they have, things they've heard others say, and also from their direct experience with the product or device. Mental models are subject to change. People refer to mental models to predict what the system, software, or product is going to do, or what they should do with it.

 Terminology can be confusing

The way I'm using the term mental model is, I believe, the most common definition, but it does not fit with at least one of the new definitions I've seen lately. In her book *Mental Models*, Indi Young uses the term in a different way. She diagrams the behavior of a particular audience doing a series of tasks, including their goals and motivations. Under the diagrams she describes what the "system" will do to match the task. She calls this entire structure a "mental model." the results seem useful, but I would not call them a mental model. It's a different use of the term.

Takeaways

﹡ People always have a mental model.

﹡ People get their mental models from past experience.

﹡ Not everyone has the same mental model.

﹡ An important reason for doing user or customer research is so you can understand the mental models of your target audience.

32 PEOPLE INTERACT WITH CONCEPTUAL MODELS

To understand why mental models are so important to design, you also have to understand what a conceptual model is and how it differs from a mental model. A mental model is the representation that a person has in his mind about the object he is interacting with. A conceptual model is the actual model that is given to the person through the design and interface of the actual product. Going back to the iPad ebook example, you have a mental model of what reading a book will be like in the iPad, how it will work, and what you can do with it. But when you sit down with the iPad, the "system" (the iPad) displays what the conceptual model of the book app actually is. There will be screens and buttons and things that happen. The actual interface is the conceptual model. Someone designed an interface and that interface is communicating to you the conceptual model of the product.

At this point you might be asking, "So? Why should I care about this mental model/conceptual model idea?" Here's why you should care: if there is a mismatch between the person's mental model and the product's conceptual model, then the product or Web site will be hard to learn, hard to use, or not accepted. How do mismatches occur? Here are some examples:

★ The designers thought they knew who would be using the interface and how much experience they had with interfaces like this, and they designed according to those assumptions without testing them, and it turns out their assumptions were wrong.

★ The audience or the product or Web site is varied. The designers designed for one persona or type of audience, and the mental model and conceptual model match for that group, but not for others.

★ There are no real designers. The conceptual model wasn't really designed at all. It's just a reflection of the underlying hardware or software or database, so the only people whose mental model it fits are the programmers. If the audience is not the programmers, then you're in trouble.

WHAT IF IT'S BRAND NEW AND I PURPOSELY WANT A MISMATCH?

What about the idea that people who have only read real, physical books will not have an accurate mental model of reading books on the iPad? In this case you know that people will not have an accurate mental model that fits. You want to change their mental model.

Sometimes you know that the mental model of the target audience will not fit the conceptual model, and instead of changing the design of the interface, you want to change people's mental model to match the conceptual model you've designed. The way to change a mental model is through training. You can use a short training video to change their mental model before the iPad even arrives at their door. In fact, one of the best purposes of training on a new product is to adjust the audiences' mental model to fit the conceptual model of the product.

 User-centered design and mental and conceptual models

You may be familiar with the term user-centered design (UCD). A UCD process is a set of tasks and activities that interface designers and usability specialists conduct to make sure a Web site or product is easy to learn and use. In my view, the UCD process is one-sided in that it is primarily about understanding what the users' mental models are (with task analysis, observations, interviews, and so on); *or* designing a conceptual model to fit the users' mental model (interface design, iterations, validation testing, and such).

Takeaways

* Design the conceptual model purposefully. Don't let it "bubble up" from the technology.

* The secret to designing an intuitive user experience is making sure that the conceptual model of your product matches, as much as possible, the mental models of your audience. If you get that right, you will have created a positive and useful experience.

* If you have a brand new product that you know will not match anyone's mental model, you'll need to provide training to prepare people to create a new mental model.

33 PEOPLE PROCESS INFORMATION BEST IN STORY FORM

One day, many years ago, I found myself in front of a classroom full of user interface designers who did not want to be there. Their boss had told them they had to attend the talk I was giving. I knew that many or most of them thought the class was a waste of time, and knowing that was making me nervous. I decided to be brave and forge ahead. Certainly my great content would grab their attention, right? I took a deep breath, smiled, and with a strong voice, I started the session with a big, "Hello, everyone. I'm certainly glad to be here." More than half the class wasn't even looking at me. They were reading their e-mails and writing out to-do lists. One guy had the morning newspaper open and was reading that. It was one of those moments where seconds seem like hours.

I thought to myself in panic, "What am I going to do?" Then I had an idea. "Let me tell you a story," I said. At the word story everyone's head jerked up and all eyes were on me. I knew I only had a few seconds to start a story that would hold their attention.

"It was 1988 and a team of Navy officers were staring at a computer screen. Something had just appeared on the radar in protected air space. They had orders to shoot down any unknown aircraft. Was this an unknown aircraft? Was it a military plane? Was it a commercial airliner? They had two minutes to decide what to do." I had them! Everyone was interested and riveted. I finished the story, which nicely made my point about why it can be so important that they should care about designing usable interfaces that avoid user uncertainty, and we were off to a great start. The rest of the day flew by, everyone was interested and engaged, and I got some of my best teacher evaluations ever. Now I make sure to use that magic phrase, "Let me tell you a story," at least once in every talk I give or class I teach.

You may have realized that what I did in the paragraph above was tell a story. Stories are very powerful. They grab and hold attention. But they do more than that. They also help people process information and they imply causation.

TRIED-AND-TRUE STORY FORMATS

Aristotle identified the basic structure of stories, and many people have expounded on his ideas since. One model is the basic three-act structure: beginning, middle, and end. This may not sound very unusual, but when Aristotle came up with it over two thousand years ago it was probably pretty radical.

In the beginning you introduce your audience to the setting, the characters, and the situation or conflict. In the story above I introduced you to the setting (I had to give a class), the characters (me and students), and the conflict (the students don't want to be there).

My story was very short, so the middle part was short too. In the middle part of a story, there are typically obstacles and conflicts that the main character has to overcome. These are usually somewhat resolved, but not completely resolved. In my story above the main character tried her usual opening and it failed. Then she started to panic.

In the end of the story the conflict comes to a climax and then is resolved. In my story above I thought of what to do (tell a story to the class), which I did, and which succeeded.

This is just a basic outline. There are many variations and plots that can be added and woven in.

CLASSIC STORIES

There are many stories that appear over and over in literature and in movies. Here are some of the popular themes that have been identified:

- ★ The Great Journey
- ★ Coming of Age
- ★ The Sacrifice
- ★ The Epic Battle
- ★ The Fall from Grace

- ★ Love
- ★ Fate
- ★ Revenge
- ★ The Trick
- ★ Mystery

STORIES IMPLY CAUSATION

Stories may create causation when none is there. Because stories usually involve some form of chronological narrative (first this happens, next this happens), they imply causation even where none exists. Christopher Chabris and Daniel Simons give this example in their book *The Invisible Gorilla* (2010). Look at these two passages:

Joey's big brother punched him again and again. The next day his body was covered by bruises.

Joey's crazy mother became furiously angry with him. The next day his body was covered by bruises.

In the first passage you don't need to assume much. Joey got punched and he has bruises. He got the bruises from being punched. In the second passage the inference is not quite so clear. Research shows that your brain will actually take a little bit longer to ponder the second paragraph. Yet most people will conclude that Joey has bruises because of his mother, even though the passage doesn't say that. In fact, if you ask people later to remember the passage, they will believe that they read in the story that Joey's mother actually hit him, even though that is not what the paragraph says.

People are quick to assign causality. Just as the visual cortex is filling in what you see to find and detect patterns (see the "How People See" chapter), our thought processes do the same thing. You are always looking for causation. Your brain assumes you have been given all the pertinent information and that there is causation. Stories make it even easier to make this causal leap.

STORIES ARE IMPORTANT IN ALL COMMUNICATIONS

Sometimes clients say to me, "Stories are fine at some Web sites, but not the one I'm working on now. I'm designing the Web site for the company's annual report. Stories aren't appropriate there; it's just financial information." Not true. There are appropriate stories you can use any time you are trying to communicate.

Medtronic is a medical technology company. Take a look at their annual report. (The online version is the same as the print version: http://216.139.227.101/interactive/mdc2010/). The cover of the report is a high-quality photo of Antoinette Walters, a patient who was helped by one of Medtronic's products. Later in the report there is a short story about Antoinette:

"Antoinette Walters, shown here and on the cover, had such a severe lumbar scoliosis that the pain incapacitated her, and the deformity was progressively getting worse. Then she underwent spinal fusion surgery using Medtronic spinal products to correct the alignment. Today, Antoinette's spine is much straighter, her pain is virtually gone, and she is several inches taller."

Antoinette's is not the only story in the annual report. Sprinkled in with the financial information are high-quality photos as well as stories about people like Antoinette and employees who invented various technologies. The stories make the rest of the information in the report more interesting, and also create a link between the financial numbers and the stated mission of the company.

Takeaways

* Stories are the natural way people process information.

* Use a story if you want people to make a causal leap.

* Stories aren't just for fun. No matter how dry you think your information is, using stories will make it understandable, interesting, and memorable.

34 PEOPLE LEARN BEST FROM EXAMPLES

Let's say you're a marketing person and you want to email your customers about a new product offering. Take a minute to glance through some directions on how to build an e-mail campaign using the MailChimp service we discussed earlier:

1. From the Dashboard or the Campaign Tab click on the big ol' "Create Campaign" button and select the type of campaign you'd like to create (start with regular ol' campaign.).

2. On Step 1 of the Campaign Builder, select the list you'd like to send to. Once you've selected the list use the "next" option to move forward, or click "send to entire list".

3. On Step 2 of the Campaign Builder, you will have the options to name your campaign, set up a subject line, from name reply-to email and personalize your "To:" field with *|MERGETAGS|*. You will also find your options for tracking, authentication, analytics tracking and social sharing. (Use the "next" and "back" options to navigate through the steps (not your browser's back button)).

4. Select a Template for your email by clicking on "pre-designed", "autoconnect", "premium", or "start from scratch", etc (to get a basic template layout that you can fully customize) under the templates heading. Templates you've set up and saved will live under "my templates". If you're providing your own code use the "paste/import HTML" or "import from URL" options. If you want to create an editable (or non-editable) Template for your clients, choose "code custom templates".

5. Once you choose your template you'll remain on Step 3 of the Campaign Builder. The content editor is where you will edit your styles and content. Click on "show style editor" to bring up the style options.

6. With the Style Editor visible and you'll have options to edit the styles for each section. Here the "Body" tab is selected and the "title style" subheading has been clicked. This will allow you to set the line height, font size and more for this section.

7. Click anywhere inside the dotted red borders to bring up the content editor box.

8. After you click save wait for your content to refresh then click on the "next" option. Our plain text generator will automagically create the plain text version from your HTML version. Just look this version over to make sure it looks the way you like and click "next" to move to the last step of the Campaign Builder.

9. Step 5 of the Campaign Builder is a "pre-delivery checklist". If we see anything missing on your campaign you'll be alerted in red on this screen. Click on "edit" to be taken directly back to any area that needs attention.

   You can preview the campaign once more by clicking on the "pop up preview" button.

   Then we recommend sending tests to several email addresses to see how the campaign looks in your recipient's inboxes. If everything looks good, you can schedule or send out your campaign.

Long and difficult to understand, right? Luckily this is *not* how the information is actually presented at MailChimp. The text is the same, but it is combined with screen shots to show an example of what the text is talking about. **Figure 34.1** shows a portion of what the screen really looks like, with text and picture together.

FIGURE 34.1 MailChimp (mailchimp.com) uses pictures to give examples of the steps. (*From MailChimp. MailChimp is a trademark of The Rocket Science Group, LLC.*)

Screen shots or pictures are not the only way to provide examples. At the MailChimp site there are also links to videos that walk you through the same steps (**Figure 34.2**). Video is one of the most effective ways to give examples online. Videos combine movement, sound, and vision, and don't require reading, so they are attention-getting and engaging.

FIGURE 34.2 MailChimp also uses videos to give examples. (*From MailChimp. MailChimp is a trademark of The Rocket Science Group, LLC.*)

Takeaways

∗ People learn best by example. Don't just tell people what to do. Show them.

∗ Use pictures and screen shots to show by example.

∗ Better yet, use short videos as examples.

35 PEOPLE ARE DRIVEN TO CREATE CATEGORIES

If you're between the ages of 5 and 60 and grew up with a television in the U.S., you probably know what I mean if I say, "One of these things is not like the other." This is a snippet from the popular children's show *Sesame Street*.

 Watch the *Sesame Street* video

If you don't know what I am talking about, you can view YouTube clips, for example, http://bit.ly/eCSFKB.

The purpose of this *Sesame Street* lesson is to teach young children how to notice differences, and essentially how to start to learn to categorize.

Interestingly, it's probably unnecessary, and perhaps even ineffective, to try and teach children how to create categories for two reasons:

★ People naturally create categories. Just as learning a native language happens naturally, so does learning to categorize the world around us.

★ Categorizing doesn't emerge as a skill until about age seven. Thinking about categories just doesn't make sense to children before that. After age seven, however, kids become fascinated with categorizing information.

PEOPLE LOVE TO CATEGORIZE

If you've ever conducted a card-sorting exercise while doing research for Web site design, then you've had the experience of watching how avidly people approach the task. In card sorting, you typically give someone a stack of cards. On each card is a word or phrase about something they would find at the Web site. For example, if you're designing a Web site that sells camping equipment, then you might have a set of cards that say things like: tents, stoves, backpack, returns, shipping, help. In a card-sorting exercise, you give people the cards and ask them to arrange the cards into whatever groups or categories make sense to them. You can have several people do the task, then analyze the groupings, and have data from which to build the organization of your Web site. I've done this many times, including using it as an exercise in classes I teach. It's one of the most engaging tasks I have people do. Everyone gets very involved in this exercise, because people like to create categories. The whole field of information architecture is about how to organize information into categories.

IF YOU DON'T PROVIDE CATEGORIES, PEOPLE WILL CREATE THEIR OWN

Just as the visual cortex imposes patterns on what we see, whether or not there are really patterns there (see the "How People See" chapter), people will impose categories when they're confronted with large amounts of information. People use categorization as a way to make sense of the world around them, especially when they feel over-whelmed with information.

WHO ORGANIZES DOESN'T MATTER AS MUCH AS *HOW WELL* IT'S ORGANIZED

While working on my master's thesis at Penn State, I conducted research on whether people would remember information better if it was organized by other people or if they organized it themselves. Basically what I found was that it didn't really matter. What mattered most was how *well* it was organized. The more organized the information, the better people remembered it. Some people (those who measured high on "locus of control" measures) preferred to organize the information in their own way, but self-orga-nization versus other organization schemes didn't really matter as long as the informa-tion was well organized.

Takeaways

✳ People like to put things into categories.

✳ If there is a lot of information and it is not in categories, people will feel overwhelmed and try to organize the information on their own.

✳ It's always a good idea to organize information for your audience as much as possible. Keep in mind the four-item rule from the "How People Remember" chapter.

✳ It's useful to get input from people on what organization schemes make the most sense to them, but the critical thing is that you organize the material. What you call things is often more important than how you have it organized.

✳ If you're designing sites for children under age seven, any organization into categories you are doing is probably more for the adults in that child's world, not for the child.

---

36 TIME IS RELATIVE

Has this ever happened to you? You're traveling to visit friends. It's two hours to get there and two hours to get back, but the trip there feels much longer.

In the interesting book, *The Time Paradox* (2009), Philip Zimbardo and John Boyd discuss how our experience of time is relative, not absolute. There are time illusions, just like there are visual illusions. Zimbardo reports on research that shows that the more mental processing you do, the more time you think has elapsed. Related to the progressive disclosure discussed earlier in this chapter, if people have to stop and think at each step of a task, they'll feel that the task is taking too long. The mental processing makes the amount of time seem longer.

The perception of time and your reaction to it are also greatly influenced by predictability and expectations. Let's say you're editing video on your computer. You've just clicked the button to produce the video file from your edits. Will you be frustrated by how long it takes to produce the video? If you do this task often, and it normally takes 3 minutes, then 3 minutes will not seem like a long time. If there is a progress indicator, then you know what to expect. You'll go pour yourself a cup of coffee and come back. But if it sometimes takes 30 seconds and sometimes takes 5 minutes, and you don't know which one it's going to be this time, then you will be very frustrated if it takes 3 minutes. Three minutes will seem much longer than it usually does.

IF PEOPLE FEEL PRESSED FOR TIME, THEY WON'T STOP TO HELP SOMEONE

In the "Good Samaritan" research by John Darley and C. Batson (1973), Princeton seminary students were asked to prepare a speech on either jobs for seminary graduates or the parable of the Good Samaritan. The parable is about several holy men who pass someone in need but don't stop to help. The Samaritan comes upon the person in need and does stop and help him. In the research study, the seminary students were asked to prepare their talks, and then they were told to go to a building across campus and give the talk. The experimenter gave the participants different instructions, depending on whether they were in the Low, Intermediate, or High Hurry category:

★ **Low Hurry**: "It'll be a few minutes before they're ready for you, but you might as well head on over. If you have to wait over there, it shouldn't be long."

★ **Intermediate Hurry**: "The assistant is ready for you, so please go right over."

★ **High Hurry**: "Oh, you're late. They were expecting you a few minutes ago. You'd better get moving. The assistant should be waiting for you so you'd better hurry. It should only take a minute."

Each student was then given a 3 x 5 card with instructions about where to go. The instructions took them past someone who was part of the experiment, and this person was huddled and coughing and groaning in an alley on campus. The question was, how many people would stop and offer help? Would it matter what talk they had been preparing to give? Would it matter what instructions they were given on whether to hurry or not?

What percentage of people stopped to help?

★ **Low hurry:** 63 percent

★ **Intermediate hurry:** 45 percent

★ **High hurry:** 10 percent

The type of talk the participants had prepared for (jobs versus the Good Samaritan parable) didn't make a significant difference in whether they stopped to help, but how much of a hurry they were in did.

EXPECTATIONS CHANGE OVER TIME

Ten years ago if it took 20 seconds for a Web site to load, we didn't think much of it. But these days if it takes more than 3 seconds you get impatient. There's one Web site I go to regularly that takes 12 seconds to load. It seems like an eternity.

 Time mechanisms in your body

Rao (2001) used fMRI images of the brain to show that there are two areas that process information about time: the basal ganglia (deep inside the brain where dopamine is stored), and the parietal lobe (on the surface of the right side of the brain). There are also some time functions built into each cell of the body.

Takeaways

∗ Always provide progress indicators so people know how much time something is going to take.

∗ If possible, make the amount of time it takes to do a task or bring up information consistent, so people can adjust their expectations accordingly.

∗ To make a process seem shorter, break it up into steps and have people think less. It's mental processing that makes something seem to take a long time.

37 THERE ARE FOUR WAYS TO BE CREATIVE

Have you heard someone say, "Oh, John—he's so creative! I wish I was creative like that." It makes it sound as if creativity is a natural skill or talent, like the ability to sing or paint. Other times people say, "I'm going to a seminar to learn how to be more creative." That makes it sound as if creativity is a skill that anyone can learn. So, which is it? Well, both and neither.

Arne Dietrich (2004) wrote a paper on creativity from a brain and neuroscience point of view. Dietrich identifies four types of creativity with corresponding brain activities:

★ Deliberate and cognitive creativity

★ Deliberate and emotional creativity

★ Spontaneous and cognitive creativity

★ Spontaneous and emotional creativity

Think of it like a matrix, as shown in **Figure 37.1**.

	Cognitive	Emotional
Deliberate	Thomas Edison	Therapeutic A-ha Moment
Spontaneous	Newton and the apple	Artists, Musicians

FIGURE 37.1 Four kinds of creativity

Creativity can be either emotionally or cognitively based, and it can also be spontaneous or deliberate. That gives you the four types.

DELIBERATE AND COGNITIVE CREATIVITY

Deliberate and cognitive creativity is the kind that comes from sustained work in a discipline. For example, Thomas Edison, the inventor of the electric light bulb as we know it, was a deliberate and cognitive creator. He ran experiment after experiment before he came up with an invention. In addition to the light bulb, Thomas Edison invented the phonograph and the motion picture camera. He held 1,093 U.S. patents, and more in Europe and the U.K. Some of his famous quotes include:

> *I am not discouraged, because every wrong attempt discarded is another step forward.*

> *I have not failed. I've just found 10,000 ways that won't work.*

> *Many of life's failures are men who did not realize how close they were to success when they gave up.*

Edison is a great example of someone who used deliberate and cognitive creativity. According to Dietrich, this type of creativity comes from the prefrontal cortex (PFC). The PFC is right behind your forehead. It's not that the PFC is where creative thought takes place; it's more that the PFC allows you to do two things:

★ Pay focused attention.

★ Make connections among bits of information you've stored in other parts of your brain.

For deliberate, cognitive creativity to occur, you need to have a pre-existing body of knowledge about one or more particular topics. When you're being deliberatively and cognitively creative, you're putting together existing information in new and novel ways.

DELIBERATE AND EMOTIONAL CREATIVITY

I remember a moment many years ago when I was having a series of crises. A long-term relationship had just ended in a difficult way. I had moved to a new city where I did not know anyone. I had started a job I wasn't sure I liked. I had rented an apartment that I couldn't really afford, and I was sleeping on a mattress on the floor because I couldn't afford to buy furniture. Then I discovered the apartment was infested with fleas. I took all my clothes to the laundromat (I couldn't afford a washer or dryer either), and when I went back to retrieve them someone had stolen them. That was the last straw.

I remember sitting quietly in my office. I had to figure out why all these things were happening. Why did I seem to be making a series of bad decisions? Then I had an *a-ha* moment. In the ten years before the current crisis, I had some tough times, including both of my parents dying. I had to be strong and independent and take care of myself. I had a belief that said, "I am a strong person. I can handle any crisis." I realized that I was making decisions that would eventually cause more crises, at least partly so I could overcome them to prove to myself that I was strong.

I decided right then to change my belief. I said out loud: "My life is easy and graceful." I walked across the hall and asked a fellow coworker if I could stay in her apartment for a few weeks until I found another place. I called my landlord and got out of the lease on the flea-infested, too expensive apartment, and began to make decisions that would make my life easier.

That is an example of deliberate, emotional creativity. This type of creativity also involves the PFC. That is the deliberate part. But instead of focusing attention on a particular area of knowledge or expertise, people who engage in deliberate, emotional creativity have *a-ha* moments having to do with feelings and emotions. The amygdala is where emotions and feelings are processed, in particular, the basic emotions of love, hate, fear, and so on. Interestingly, the PFC is not connected to the amygdala. But there is another part of your brain that also has to do with emotions. That is the cingulate cortex. This part of the brain works with more complex feelings that are related to how you interact with others and your place in the world. And the cingulated cortex is connected to the PFC.

SPONTANEOUS AND COGNITIVE CREATIVITY

Imagine you're working on a problem that you can't seem to solve. Maybe you're trying to figure out how to staff a project at work, and you just don't see how to free up the right people to do the project. You don't have the answer yet, but it's lunchtime and you're meeting a friend and need to run some errands, too. On your way back from errands and lunch, you're walking down the street and suddenly you get a flash of insight about how to staff the project. This is an example of spontaneous and cognitive creativity.

Spontaneous and cognitive creativity involves the basal ganglia of the brain. This is where dopamine is stored, and it is a part of the brain that operates outside your conscious awareness. During spontaneous and cognitive creativity, the conscious brain stops working on the problem, and this gives the unconscious part of the brain a chance to work on it instead. If a problem requires "out of the box" thinking, then you need to remove it temporarily from conscious awareness. By doing a different, unrelated activity, the PFC is able to connect information in new ways via your unconscious mental processing. The story about Isaac Newton thinking of gravity while watching a falling apple is an example of spontaneous and cognitive creativity. Notice that this type of creativity does require an existing body of knowledge. That is the cognitive part.

SPONTANEOUS AND EMOTIONAL CREATIVITY

Spontaneous and emotional creativity comes from the amygdala. The amygdala is where basic emotions are processed. When the conscious brain and the PFC are at rest, spontaneous ideas and creations can emerge. This is the kind of creativity that great artists and musicians possess. Often these kinds of spontaneous and emotional creative moments are quite powerful, such as an epiphany, or a religious experience.

There is not specific knowledge necessary (it's not cognitive) for this type of creativity, but there is often skill (writing, artistic, musical) needed to create something from the spontaneous and emotional creative idea.

 When you're stuck, go to sleep

Sara Mednick, a neuroscientist at the University of California, San Diego, wrote a book called *Take a Nap, Change Your Life* (2006), based on the research she and others have done on creativity and problem solving. In a typical experiment, she gave participants puzzles to solve. Before they solved the puzzles she would have them take a nap. Participants who went into REM sleep during the nap solved 40 percent more puzzles after the nap than when they worked on the puzzles in the morning after a full night's sleep. People who just rested or napped without REM sleep actually did worse.

Ullrich Wagner (2004) conducted an experiment where participants were given a boring task of changing a long list of number strings into a new set of number strings. To do this they had to use complicated algorithms. There was a shortcut, but it involved seeing a link between the different sets of numbers. Less than 25 percent of the participants found the shortcut, even after several hours. But if people slept in between, then almost 60 percent of the participants found the shortcut.

Takeaways

∗ There are different ways to be creative. If you're designing an experience that is supposed to foster creativity, decide first which type of creativity you are talking about and design for that.

∗ Deliberate and cognitive creativity requires a high degree of knowledge and lots of time. If you want people to show this type of creativity, you have to make sure you are providing enough prerequisite information. You need to give resources of where people can go to get the information they need to be creative. You also need to give them enough time to work on the problem.

(Continues)

Takeaways (continued)

✳ Deliberate and emotional creativity requires quiet time. You can provide questions or things for people to ponder, but don't expect that they will be able to come up with answers quickly and just by interacting with others at a Web site. For example, creating an online support site for people with a particular problem might ultimately result in deliberate and emotional creativity, but the person will probably have to go offline and have quiet time to have the insights. Suggest that they do that and then come back online to share their insights with others.

✳ Spontaneous and cognitive creativity requires stopping work on the problem and getting away. If you are designing a Web application or site where you expect people to solve a problem with this kind of creativity, you will need to set up the problem in one stage and then have them come back a few days later with their solution.

✳ Spontaneous and emotional creativity probably can't be designed for.

✳ Remember that your own creative process for design follows these same rules. Allow yourself time to work on a creative design solution, and when you are stuck, sleep on it.

38 PEOPLE CAN BE IN A FLOW STATE

Imagine you're engrossed in some activity. It could be something physical like rock climbing or skiing, something artistic or creative like playing the piano or painting, or just an everyday activity like working on a PowerPoint presentation or teaching a class. Whatever the activity, you become totally engrossed, totally in the moment. Everything else falls away, your sense of time changes, and you almost forget who you are and where you are. What I'm describing is called a *flow state*.

The man who wrote the book on flow is Mihaly Csikszentmihalyi. He's been studying the flow state around the world for many years. Here are some facts about the flow state, the conditions that produce it, what it feels like, and how to apply the concept to your designs:

★ You have very focused attention on your task. The ability to control and focus your attention is critical. If you get distracted by anything outside the activity you're engaging in, the flow state will dissipate. If you want people to be in a flow state while using your product, minimize distractions when they are doing a particular task.

★ You're working with a specific, clear, and achievable goal in mind. Whether you're singing, fixing a bike, or running a marathon, the flow state comes about when you have a specific goal. You then keep that focused attention and only let in information that fits with the goal. Research shows that you need to feel that you have a good chance of completing the goal to get into, and hold onto, the flow state. If you think you have a good chance of failing at the goal, then the flow state will not be induced. And, conversely, if the activity is not challenging enough, then you won't hold your attention on it and the flow state will end. Make sure to build in enough challenge to hold attention, but don't make the tasks so hard that people get discouraged.

★ You receive constant feedback. To stay in the flow state, you need a constant stream of information coming in that gives you feedback as to the achievement of the goal. Make sure you are building in lots of feedback messages as people perform the tasks.

★ You have control over your actions. Control is an important condition of the flow state. You don't necessarily have to be in control, or even feel like you're in control of the entire situation, but you do have to feel that you're exercising significant control over your own actions in a challenging situation. Give people control at various points along the way.

★ Time changes. Some people report that time speeds up—they look up and hours have gone by. Others report that time slows down.

★ The self does not feel threatened. To enter a flow state, your sense of self and survival cannot feel threatened. You have to be relaxed enough to engage all of your attention on the task at hand. In fact, most people report that they lose their sense of self when they are absorbed with the task.

★ The flow state is personal. Everyone has different activities that put them in a flow state. What triggers a flow state for you is different from others.

★ The flow state crosses cultures. So far it seems to be a common human experience across all cultures with the exception of people with some mental illnesses. People who have schizophrenia, for example, have a hard time inducing or staying in a flow state, probably because they have a hard time with some of the other items above, such as focused attention, control, or the self not feeling threatened.

★ The flow state is pleasurable. People like being in the flow state.

★ The prefrontal cortex and basal ganglia are both involved. I haven't found specific research on the brain correlates of the flow state, but given that it combines time changes, pleasurable feelings, and concentrated focus, I'm guessing it involves both the prefrontal cortex, which is responsible for focused attention, as well as the basal ganglia, which is involved in dopamine production.

Takeaways

If you're trying to design for, or induce, a flow state (for example, you are a game designer):

✳ Give people control over their actions during the activity.

✳ Break up the difficulty into stages. People need to feel that the current goal is challenging, yet achievable.

✳ Give constant feedback.

✳ Minimize distractions.

39 CULTURE AFFECTS HOW PEOPLE THINK

Take a look at **Figure 39.1**. What do you notice more: the cows or the backgrounds?

FIGURE 39.1 Picture used in Hannah Chua (2005) research

The way you answer might depend on where you grew up—the West (U.S., U.K., Europe) or East Asia. In his book, *The Geography of Thought*, Richard Nisbett discusses research that shows that how we think is influenced and shaped by culture.

EAST = RELATIONSHIPS; WEST = INDIVIDUALISTIC

If you show people from the West a picture, they focus on a main or dominant fore-ground object, while people from East Asia pay more attention to context and back-ground. East Asian people who grow up in the West show the Western pattern, not the Asian pattern, thereby implying that it's culture, not genetics, that accounts for the differences.

The theory is that in East Asia, cultural norms emphasize relationships and groups. East Asians, therefore, grow up learning to pay more attention to context. Western society is more individualistic, so Westerners grow up learning to pay attention to focal objects.

Hannah Chua et al. (2005) and Lu Zihui (2008) both used the pictures in **Figure 39.1** and eye tracking to measure eye movement. They both showed that the East Asian participants spent more time with central vision on the backgrounds and the Western participants spent more time with central vision on the foreground.

CULTURAL DIFFERENCES SHOW UP IN BRAIN SCANS

Sharon Begley recently wrote an article in Newsweek on neuroscience research that also confirms the cultural effects:

"When shown complex, busy scenes, Asian-Americans and non-Asian-Americans recruited different brain regions. The Asians showed more activity in areas that process figure-ground relations—holistic context—while the Americans showed more activity in regions that recognize objects."

 Concerns about generalizing research?

If Western and Eastern people think differently, then do we have to wonder how much we can generalize psychology (or other) research results from one group to another? It's been common practice to use research subjects from only one geographical region. Now you have to wonder about the accuracy of some of this research. Does it describe only the people in that area? Fortunately there is more and more research coming out of various parts of the world, and more individual studies being conducted in multiple locations. Psychological research now is less focused on one region or group as it has been in the past.

Takeaways

✳ People from different geographical regions and cultures respond differently to photos and Web site designs. In East Asia people notice and remember the background and context more than people in the West do.

✳ If you are designing products for multiple cultures and geographical regions, then you had better conduct audience research in multiple locations.

✳ When reading psychology research, you might want to avoid generalizing the results if you know that the study participants were all from one geographical region. Be careful of overgeneralizing.

HOW PEOPLE FOCUS THEIR ATTENTION

What makes us sit up and take notice? How do you grab and hold someone's attention? How do we choose what to notice and what to pay attention to?

40 ATTENTION IS SELECTIVE

Robert Solso (2005) developed this exercise: in the paragraph below, read only the words that are bold, and ignore all the other text.

Somewhere **Among** *hidden on a* **the** *desert island* **most** *near the* **spectacular** *X islands, an* **cognitive** *old Survivor* **abilities** *contestant* **is** *has* **the** *concealed* **ability** *a box* **to** *of gold* **select** *won* **one** *in a* **message** *reward* **from** *challenge* **another. We** *Although* **do** *several hundred* **this** *people* **by** *(fans,* **focusing** *contestants,* **our** *and producers) have* **attention** *looked* **on** *for it* **certain** *they* **cues** *have* **such** *not* **as** *found* **type** *it* **style.** *Rumor* **When** *has* **we** *it* **focus** *that 300* **our** *paces* **attention** *due* **on** *west* **certain** *from* **stimuli** *tribal* **the** *council* **message** *and* **in** *then* **other** *200* **stimuli** *paces* **is** *due* **not** *north X marks* **clearly** *the spot* **identified.** *Apparently* **However** *enough* **some** *gold* **information** *can* **from** *be* **the** *had* **unattended** *to* **source** *purchase* **may** *the* **be** *very* **detected** *island!*

People are easily distracted in many situations. In fact, their attention can often be pulled away from what they're focusing on. But they can also pay attention to one thing and filter out all other stimuli. This is called selective attention.

How difficult it is to grab their attention depends on how engrossed or involved they are. For example, if they come to your Web site to shop for a gift and aren't sure what to get, it will be fairly easy to grab their attention with video, a large photo, color, or animation. **Figure 40.1** provides a good example of this.

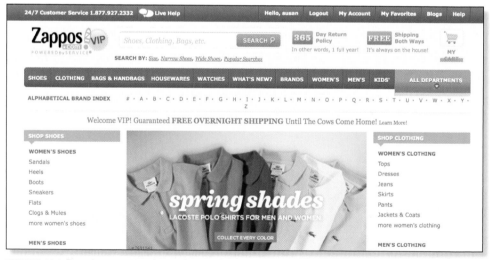

FIGURE 40.1 People pay attention to large photos and colors

On the other hand, if someone is concentrating on a particular task, such as completing the information shown in **Figure 40.2**, they're probably filtering out distractions.

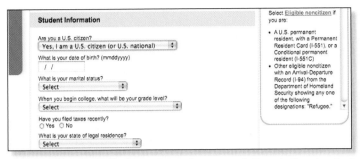

FIGURE 40.2 People filter out distractions completing challenging tasks

UNCONSCIOUS SELECTIVE ATTENTION

Imagine you're walking down a path in the woods and thinking about an upcoming business trip when you see a snake on the ground. You jump backwards. Your heart races. You're ready to run. But wait, it's not a snake; it's just a stick. You calm down and keep walking. You noticed the stick, and even responded to it, in a largely unconscious way.

My book *Neuro Web Design: What Makes Them Click?* is about unconscious mental processing. Sometimes you're aware of your conscious selective attention, like when you were reading the paragraph at the beginning of this chapter. But selective attention also operates unconsciously.

 The cocktail party

Imagine you're at a cocktail party. You're talking to the person next to you. It's noisy, but you can screen out the other conversations. Then you hear someone say your name. Your name cut through your filter and quickly came to your attention.

Takeaways

✳ People will pay attention to only one thing and ignore everything else as long as you give them specific instructions to do so, and the task doesn't take too long.

✳ A person's unconscious constantly scans the environment for certain things. These include their own name as well as messages about food, sex, and danger.

41 PEOPLE FILTER INFORMATION

Have you ever met someone who has a long-held belief that he just won't change, no matter how much evidence you show him that the belief is not tenable? People seek out and pay attention to information and cues that confirm their beliefs. They don't seek out—in fact, they ignore or even discount—information that doesn't support what they already believe.

Filtering is often useful, since it reduces the amount of information we have to pay attention to at any one time. But sometimes filtering can lead to bad choices.

In 1988 the U.S. Navy had a ship in the Persian Gulf called the USS *Vincennes*. One day, while scanning the radar screen on the ship, the crew saw an aircraft headed their way. They decided early on that the approaching aircraft was not a commercial airliner, but a hostile military plane. They shot down the plane, which did turn out to be a commercial airliner with 290 passengers and crew on board. Everyone died.

Many factors led to this erroneous conclusion. The situation was stressful (I'll cover stress in the chapter on People Make Mistakes), and the room was too dark. There were many ambiguous pieces of information that made it hard for the *Vincennes* crew to understand what they were looking at on their radar screen. Most significant, however, is what they chose to pay attention to and what they chose to ignore. Several crew members were convinced from the start that it was a hostile military plane, and from that point on they filtered all the incoming information. They had repeatedly rehearsed the training scenario on what to do when a hostile military plane entered their air space. They ignored evidence that it was a commercial plane, paid attention only to the information that supported their belief that it was a hostile military craft, and then proceeded to carry out the training scenario. All of this led them to an incorrect conclusion.

Takeaways

* Don't expect that people will necessarily pay attention to information you provide.

* Don't make assumptions. What is obvious to you as the designer may not be obvious to the people using what you've designed.

* If you think people might be filtering information, use color, size, animation, video, and sound to draw attention to what's important.

* If it's critical that people pay attention to certain information, make that information stand out 10 times more than you think is necessary.

42 WELL-PRACTICED SKILLS DON'T REQUIRE CONSCIOUS ATTENTION

When my children were growing up they took music lessons using the Suzuki method. My son studied violin, and my daughter studied piano. After attending one of my daughter's recitals, I asked her what she was thinking about while she was performing the piano sonata from memory, with no music in front of her. The dynamics of the music? When to get louder or softer? Particular notes or passages that were coming up?

She looked at me in confusion.

"Thinking?" she said. "I'm not thinking about anything. I'm just watching my fingers play the song."

It was my turn to be confused.

I turned to my son and asked, "Is that how you play the violin in a recital? Are you thinking?"

"No, of course I'm not thinking," he answered. "I'm watching my fingers play the violin, too."

The Suzuki method stresses constant repetition. Students don't have music in front of them during recitals; instead, they memorize all the pieces, many of them quite complicated. They practice their music so often, they learn how to play it without even thinking.

If a skill is practiced so much that it becomes automatic, then it can be performed with a minimum of conscious attention. If it's truly automatic then it almost allows multitasking. I say *almost* because multitasking doesn't really exist.

TOO MANY AUTOMATIC STEPS CAN LEAD TO ERRORS

Have you ever used a software application that requires you to go through a series of steps to delete an item? You have to click the item, then click the Delete button, then a window pops up and you have to click the Yes button to confirm. You need to delete about 25 files, so you position your fingers in an optimal way and start clicking. Before too long your fingers have taken over, and you aren't even thinking about what you're doing. In this type of situation it's easy to accidentally keep deleting past where you were supposed to.

Takeaways

✳ If people perform a series of steps over and over again, the action will become automatic.

✳ If you require people to perform a sequence repeatedly, make it easy to do, but realize that the trade-off is that people may make errors because they no longer are paying attention.

✳ Make it easy for people to undo not only their last action, but also an entire sequence.

✳ Rather than requiring people to perform a task over and over, consider a design where they can choose all the items they want to take action on and then perform the action on all the items at once.

43 EXPECTATIONS OF FREQUENCY AFFECT ATTENTION

Last year Farid Seif, a businessman from Houston, Texas, boarded a flight in Houston with a loaded handgun in his laptop case. He made it through security without a problem. Seif was not a terrorist. The gun was legal in Texas; he simply forgot to take it out of his laptop case before his trip.

Security at the Houston airport did not detect the gun. It should have been easily seen by security personnel looking at the x-ray scanner, but no one noticed it.

The U.S. Department of Homeland Security routinely tests the ability to pass security screening with guns, bomb parts, and other forbidden items by sending them through with undercover agents. The U.S. government won't release the figures officially, yet, but the estimate is that 70 percent of these tests fail, meaning most of the time the agents are able to get through security, like Farid Seif, with objects that are supposed to be spotted.

Why does this happen? Why do security personnel notice the bottle of lotion that is too large, but miss a loaded handgun?

 Watch a Video about Farid Seif

You can see an ABC News video on this topic at: http://abcnews.go.com/Blotter/loaded-gun-slips-past-tsa-screeners/story?id=12412458

A MENTAL MODEL ABOUT FREQUENCY

Security personnel miss the loaded handgun and bomb parts at least in part because they don't encounter them frequently. A security officer is working for hours at a time, watching people, and looking at the scanner screen. He develops an expectation about how frequently certain violations occur. For example, he probably encounters containers of hand lotion or nail clippers fairly often, and so expects to see those, and then looks for them. On the other hand, he probably doesn't encounter loaded handguns or bomb parts very often. He creates a mental model about how frequently any of these items will occur, and then, unconsciously, starts paying attention accordingly.

Andrew Bellenkes (1997) conducted research on this expectation and found that if people expect something to happen with a particular frequency, they often miss it if it happens more or less than their expectations. They have a mental model of how often something will occur and they have set their attention to that mental model.

Signal if it's infrequent and important

I use my laptop for hours every day, and most of the time it's plugged in. But sometimes I forget to plug it in and my battery gets low. There is an indicator on my screen that constantly shows that the battery power is disappearing, but if I'm at home I think I'm plugged in, and I don't notice the indicator.

Eventually (about eight percent of battery left), my computer makes a sound and a message pops up to alert me that the battery is very low. This is an example of signaling when an event is infrequent, but important. (I wish that Apple gave me the option of customizing when I want to be alerted, however. By the time I get the alert, the battery is really low. Then I run around panicked trying to find my plug or an outlet, or saving files.)

Takeaways

✳ People will build an unconscious mental model of how often an event occurs.

✳ If you're designing a product or application where people need to notice an event that rarely occurs, use a strong signal to get their attention when it does.

44 SUSTAINED ATTENTION LASTS ABOUT TEN MINUTES

Imagine you're in a meeting and someone is presenting sales figures for the last quarter. How long can she hold your attention? If the topic is of interest to you, and she is a good presenter, you can focus on the presentation about 7 to 10 minutes at most. If you're not interested in the topic or the presenter is particularly boring, then you'll lose interest much faster. **Figure 44.1** shows what the graph looks like.

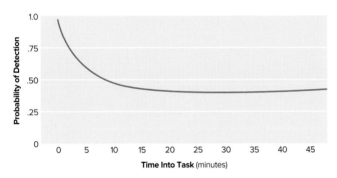

FIGURE 44.1 Attention starts to wane after 10 minutes

People can take a short break and then start over with another 7- to 10-minute period, but 7 to 10 minutes is about as long as we can pay attention to any one task.

If you're designing a Web site, you're probably designing pages that someone views for a lot less than seven minutes. You're assuming that someone comes to the page, looks for a link, and clicks on it. But sometimes you might be adding in other media, such as audio or video. These media are subject to the 7 to 10 minute rule. TED videos are typically 20 minutes long, so they're going over the limit (although they have some of the world's greatest speakers, and so might be able to stretch it). Lynda.com does a good job of keeping most of their online tutorials under 10 minutes.

Takeaways

* Assume that you have at most 7 to 10 minutes of a person's attention.

* If you must hold attention longer than 7 to 10 minutes, introduce novel information or a break.

* Keep online demos or tutorials under 7 minutes in length.

45 PEOPLE PAY ATTENTION ONLY TO SALIENT CUES

Look at the pictures of a U.S. penny in **Figure 45.1**. Which one is the real penny? Don't cheat. Try and figure it out first, before you go get a penny to check.

FIGURE 45.1 Which is the real penny?

If you live in the U.S. and use U.S. coins, then a penny is something you've probably seen a lot. But you only pay attention to certain attributes of the penny, for instance, its color and size. These are what psychologists call "salient cues." You only pay attention to what you need for the task at hand. Although there's a lot of detail on the penny, a lot of cues, the salient ones for most people are color and size. If you're a coin collector, then the salient cues are different. Salient cues for a coin collector might include the date, wording, or particular pictures.

As we saw in the chapter on "How People See," you can look at something and not really see it. Similarly, everyday you experience a lot of things through sight, sound, taste, and touch that you don't pay attention to. People are unconsciously aware that they have limited resources, and the brain therefore decides what it really needs to pay attention to and what it can ignore.

Did you guess the right penny? (It's A.)

Takeaways

∗   Decide what the salient cues are for your audience.

∗   Design so that the salient cues are obvious.

∗   Realize that people will probably only pay attention to salient cues.

46 PEOPLE CAN'T ACTUALLY MULTITASK

I know it's popular to think that you are multitasking, but the research is clear: people can't actually multitask. (There's one specific, possible exception that I'll get to in a moment.)

For many years psychology research has shown that people can attend to only one task at a time. You can only think about one thing at a time. You can only conduct one mental activity at a time. So you can talk, or you can read. You can read, or you can type. You can listen, or you can read—one thing at a time. We are pretty good at switching back and forth quickly, so we *think* we are multitasking, but in reality we are not.

ONE POSSIBLE EXCEPTION

Research has uncovered one possible exception: if you are doing a physical task that you have done very, very often, and you are very good at, then you can do that physical task while you are doing a mental task. So if you are an adult and you have learned to walk, then you can walk and talk at the same time. Well, maybe. Even walking and talking doesn't always work very well. A study by Ira Hyman (2009) showed that people talking on their cell phones while walking ran into people (literally) more often, and didn't notice what was around them. The researchers had someone in a clown suit ride a unicycle. The people talking on a cell phone were much less likely to notice or remember the clown.

 Driving while on a cell phone is an attention problem

In many parts of the U.S., it is now illegal to drive while holding a cell phone, but it is OK to use a cell phone while driving if you have a hands-free phone. There's a flaw in this thinking. It's not the holding of the phone that is a problem, it's the conversation you are having with the other person. When you have a phone conversation, your attention is on the conversation, and therefore your attention is not on driving. It's an attention problem, not a hands-free problem.

Overhearing someone talk on a cell phone is more annoying than overhearing two people in conversation

A one-sided conversation (or halfalogue) uses more of your mental resources, because the information is less predictable. You're in suspense wondering what you're missing in the other half of the conversation. Lauren Emberson (2010) tested participants on different mental tasks. They performed much better on tasks when they heard both sides of a cell-phone call than when they heard a halfalogue. The researchers controlled for acoustic factors (quality of the sound, and so on), so they concluded that this difference occurs because the halfalogue is unpredictable. Because participants are thinking about the half of the conversation they're missing, they are not paying attention to the task at hand.

DO AGE AND MULTITASKING EXPERIENCE MAKE A DIFFERENCE?

Eyal Ophir and Clifford Nass (2009) conducted a series of studies on college students and determined that they were no better at multitasking than the general population. They developed a questionnaire, which asked people how many different media they use simultaneously. They then picked people who were at either end of the spectrum: heavy media multitaskers (HMMs) and light media multitaskers (LMMs).

Next, they had people from each group perform several tasks. For example, they showed people two red rectangles alone, or two red rectangles surrounded by four or six blue rectangles. These objects were flashed twice, and the participants had to decide whether the two red rectangles had moved from the first flash to the second. They were supposed to ignore the blue rectangles.

What they found was opposite to what they thought they would find. The LMMs were able to ignore the blue rectangles, but the HMMs had a harder time ignoring the blue rectangles, and therefore did much worse on the task. Next they tried tasks that involved letters and numbers. The results were always the same: the HMMs were actually more distracted by irrelevant stimuli than the LMMs, and performed poorly on the tasks.

 Watch a video on multitasking research

To watch a video about the Ophir and Nass research: http://www.youtube.com/watch?v=2zuDXzVYZ68

Takeaways

✳ People will tell you they can multitask but they actually can't.

✳ Those who describe themselves as great multitaskers are probably the worst at it.

✳ Young people do not multitask better than older people.

✳ Avoid forcing people to multitask. It is difficult for them to do two things at once, for example, have a conversation with a customer while filling out a form on a computer or tablet device. If people must multitask, pay particular attention to the usability of the form.

✳ If you require people to multitask, expect them to make lots of errors and build in ways for them to fix errors afterwards.

✳ Driving while having a cell phone conversation is like driving under the influence of alcohol.

47 DANGER, FOOD, SEX, MOVEMENT, FACES, AND STORIES GET THE MOST ATTENTION

Here's what grabs attention the most:

★ Anything that moves (for example, video or blinking)

★ Pictures of human faces, especially if they are looking right at you

★ Pictures of food, sex, or danger

★ Stories

★ Loud noises (covered in Number 48)

WHY PEOPLE CAN'T RESIST PAYING ATTENTION TO FOOD, SEX, AND DANGER

Have you ever wondered why traffic always slows when people are driving by an accident? Do you moan about the fact that people are attracted by the gruesome, and yet find that you glance over too as you drive by? Well, it's not really your fault that you (and everybody else) can't resist looking at scenes of danger. It's your *old brain* telling you to PAY ATTENTION.

You have three brains

In *Neuro Web Design: What Makes Them Click?* I talk about the idea that you really don't have one brain, you have three. The *new brain* is the conscious, reasoning, logical brain that you think you know best; the *mid-brain* is the part that processes emotions, and the *old brain* is the part that is most interested in your survival. From an evolutionary perspective, the old brain developed first. In fact, that part of our brain is very similar to that of a reptile, which is why some people call it the "reptilian brain."

Can I eat it? Can I have sex with it? Will it kill me?

The job of your old brain is to constantly scan the environment and answer the questions: "Can I eat it? Can I have sex with it? Will it kill me?" That's really all the old brain cares about (**Figure 47.1**). When you think about it, this is important. Without food you'll die, without sex the species won't survive, and if you're killed the other two questions don't matter. So animal brains developed early on to care intensely about these three topics. As animals evolved they developed other capacities (emotions, logical thought), but they retained a part of their brain to always be scanning for these three critical things.

FIGURE 47.1 Looking at food is one of the things your old brain can't resist. Photo by Guthrie Weinschenk.

So you can't resist

What this means is that you just can't resist noticing food, sex, or danger, no matter how hard you try not to. It's the old brain working. You don't necessarily have to do anything once you notice; for example, you don't have to eat the chocolate cake when you see it, you don't have to flirt with the attractive woman who walked into the room, and you don't have to run away from the big, scary guy who walked in the room with the good-looking woman. But you *will* notice all of those things whether you want to or not.

⭐ **Your attention is riveted by pictures of people**

People are hard-wired to pay attention to faces. Read the chapter on "How We See" for more details on the parts of the brain that process faces.

Takeaways

 It may not always be appropriate to use food, sex, or danger in your Web page or software application, but if you do they'll get a lot of attention.

✳ Use images of up-close faces.

✳ Use stories as much as you can, even for what you think is factual information.

48 LOUD NOISES STARTLE AND GET ATTENTION

If you want to get someone's attention with a sound, **Table 48.1** describes some choices and when to use each one (adapted from Deatherage, 1972).

TABLE 48.1 How To Get Attention With Sounds

Audio alarm	Intensity	Attention-getting ability
Foghorn	Very high	Good, but not if there is a lot of other low frequency noise
Regular horn	High	Good
Whistle	High	Good, but only if intermittent
Siren	High	Good if pitch rises and falls
Bell	Medium	Good when there is other low-frequency noise
Buzzer	Low to medium	Good
Chimes or gong	Low to medium	Fair

PEOPLE HABITUATE TO STIMULI

Have you visited with someone who had a clock that chimed every hour? You're lying in bed about to doze off, and there goes that darn clock again. "How can anyone get any sleep in this house?" you wonder. Yet everyone who lives in the house sleeps just fine. They have habituated to the sound of the clock chimes. Because they hear it every hour, they don't pay attention to it anymore.

Your unconscious mind is constantly surveying your environment making sure there is nothing in it that is dangerous. That's why anything new or novel in the environment will get your attention. But if the same signal occurs again and again, eventually your unconscious mind decides it is not new anymore, and therefore starts to ignore it.

Takeaways

✳ If you're designing an application, you may have control over the sounds that occur when a people take certain actions, for example, making a mistake, reaching a goal, or donating money.

✳ Pick a sound that is appropriate to the amount of attention you need. Save the high-attention sounds for when it's really important, for example, if people are about to format their hard drives, or take an action that can't be undone.

✳ If you use sounds to get attention, then consider changing them so that people will not habituate and the sounds will continue to be attention-getting.

49 FOR PEOPLE TO PAY ATTENTION TO SOMETHING, THEY MUST FIRST PERCEIVE IT

For you to pay attention to something, you must be able to sense and perceive it. Here are some examples of the sensitivity of your senses:

Sight: If you're standing at a high point in total darkness, you can see a candle 30 miles away.

Sound: If you're in a very quiet room, you can hear a watch ticking 20 feet away.

Smell: You can smell a drop of perfume in about 800 square feet of space.

Touch: You can feel a human hair on your skin.

Taste: You can taste a teaspoon of sugar in two gallons of water.

SIGNAL DETECTION THEORY

If you can't find your watch, and you're trying to figure out where you left it, then you'll hear it ticking if you're within 20 feet of it. But what if you aren't looking for your watch? What if you're unconcerned with your watch, and instead you're thinking about what to have for dinner. In that case you may not even realize that there's a watch ticking at all.

Detecting something is not necessarily simple. Your senses may perceive a stimulus, but that doesn't mean that you're paying attention to it.

Sensitivity and bias

Imagine you're expecting someone to come by and pick you up. They're late, and you keep running to the door thinking you heard the car in the driveway, even though you didn't.

Whether you perceive something or not depends on more than just the stimulus being there. In fact, sometimes the stimulus is there and you miss it, and sometimes it's not there and you think you hear or see it.

Scientists call this *signal detection theory*. There are four possible outcomes, as shown in **Figure 49.1**.

This is not just a conceptual idea. There are real cases that signal detection researchers study. Take, for example, a radiologist who is looking at dozens of medical images every day. The radiologist has to decide if there is a small dot on the image and if it's cancer or not. If she sees a cancer dot when none is there (false alarm), then the patient may have surgery, radiation therapy, and chemotherapy when it's unnecessary. On the other hand, if she misses a cancer dot that was actually there, then the patient may die because treatment was not given early enough. Psychologists study the different conditions that make it more likely for people to detect a signal accurately.

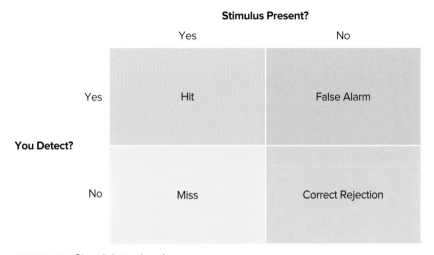

FIGURE 49.1 Signal detection theory

HOW TO APPLY SIGNAL DETECTION THEORY

Let's say you're designing a new system for air traffic controllers to see how many planes are near each other in the air space. You don't want misses, so you turn up the signal (use brighter lights, more sound) to make sure the controller doesn't miss the signal. If you were designing the screen to show x-ray results for the radiologist, you would turn down the signal a little bit to avoid false alarms.

Takeaways

＊ If you're designing for a particular task, think about the four quadrants of the signal detection chart. Is it more damaging for people to have a false alarm or a miss?

＊ Think about what you may need to do with your design based on the four quadrants of the signal detection chart. If a false alarm is worse, then tone down the signal. If a miss is worse, then make the signal stronger.

WHAT
MOTIVATES
PEOPLE

New research on motivation reveals that some of the supposedly tried-and-true methods for getting and keeping people motivated may have been tried, but they're not quite true.

50 PEOPLE ARE MORE MOTIVATED AS THEY GET CLOSER TO A GOAL

You're given a frequent buyer card for your local coffee shop. Each time you buy a cup of coffee you get a stamp on your card. When the card is filled, you get a free cup of coffee. Here are two different scenarios:

★ **Card A:** The card has 10 boxes for the stamps, and when you get the card, all the boxes are blank.

★ **Card B:** The card has 12 boxes for the stamps, and when you get the card the first two boxes are already stamped.

Question: How long will it take you to get the card filled up? Will it take longer or shorter for scenario A versus scenario B? After all, you have to buy 10 cups of coffee in both scenarios in order to get the free coffee. So does it make a difference which card you use?

The answer, apparently, is yes. You'll fill up the card faster with Card B than with Card A. And the reason is called the *goal-gradient effect*.

The goal-gradient effect was first studied in 1934 by Clark Hull using rats. He found that rats that were running a maze to get food at the end would run faster as they got to the end of the maze.

The goal-gradient effect says that you will accelerate your behavior as you progress closer to your goal. The coffee reward card scenarios I describe above were part of a research study by Ran Kivetz (2006) to see if people would act like the rats did in the original 1934 study. And the answer is, yes, they do. In addition to the coffee shop study, Kivetz found that people would go to a Web site more frequently and rate more songs during each visit as they got closer to a reward goal at the site.

The Dropbox Web site (**Figure 50.1**) shows how close you are to reaching a goal that gives you extra storage space. As you get closer to the goal, you'll be more motivated to take the one or two steps left to reach it.

 People focus on what's left more than what's completed

> Minjung Koo and Ayelet Fishbach (2010) conducted research to see which would motivate people more to reach a goal: a) focusing on what they'd already completed, or b) focusing on what remained to accomplish. The answer was b—people were more motivated to continue when they focused on what was left to do.

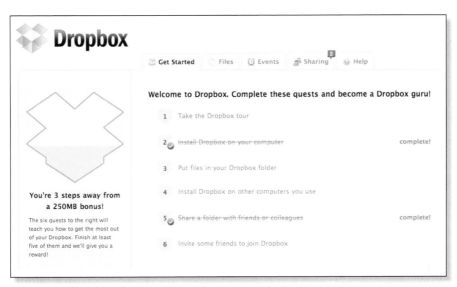

FIGURE 50.1 Dropbox shows you how close you are to the goal

Takeaways

* The shorter the distance to the goal, the more motivated people are to reach it. People are even more motivated when the end is in sight.

* You can get this extra motivation even with the illusion of progress, as in the coffee card B example in this section. There really isn't any progress (you still have to buy 10 coffees), but it seems like there has been some progress so it has the same effect.

* People enjoy being part of a reward program. When compared to customers who were not part of the program, Kivetz found that the customers with reward cards smiled more, chatted longer with café employees, said "thank you" more often, and left a tip more often.

* Motivation and purchases plummet right after the goal is reached. This is called a *post-reward resetting phenomenon*. If you have a second reward level people won't initially be very motivated to reach that second reward.

* You're most at risk of losing your customer right after a reward is reached.

51 VARIABLE REWARDS ARE POWERFUL

If you studied psychology in the twentieth century, you may remember B. F. Skinner and his work on operant conditioning. Skinner studied whether behavior increased or decreased based on how often, and in what manner, a *reinforcement* (reward) was given.

WHAT THE CASINOS KNOW

Let's say you put a rat in a cage with a bar. If the rat presses the bar he gets a food pellet. The food pellet is called the reinforcement. But what if you set it up so that the rat does not get the food pellet every time he presses the bar. Skinner tested out various scenarios, and found that the frequency with which you gave the food pellet, and whether you give it based on elapsed time or bar presses, affected how often the rat would press the bar. Here's a synopsis of the different schedules:

★ **Interval schedules.** You provide a food pellet after a certain interval of time has passed, for example, five minutes. The rat gets a food pellet the first time he presses the bar after five minutes is up.

★ **Ratio schedules.** Instead of basing the reinforcement on time, you base it on the number of bar presses. The rat gets a food pellet after every 10 bar presses.

There's another twist. You can have fixed or variable variations on each schedule. If it's a fixed schedule, then you keep the same interval or ratio, for example, every five minutes or every 10 presses. If it's variable, then you vary the time or ratio, but it averages out; for example, sometimes you provide the reinforcement after two minutes, sometimes after eight minutes, but it averages out to five minutes.

So altogether there are four possible schedules:

★ **Fixed interval.** Reinforcement is based on time and the time interval is always the same.

★ **Variable interval.** Reinforcement is based on time. The amount of time varies, but it averages to a particular time.

★ **Fixed ratio.** Reinforcement is based on the number of bar presses, and the number is always the same.

★ **Variable ratio.** Reinforcement is based on the number of bar presses. The number varies, but it averages to a particular ratio.

It turns out that rats (and people) behave in predictable ways based on the schedule you're using. **Figure 51.1** shows a chart of the kind of behavior you'll get based on the type of schedule.

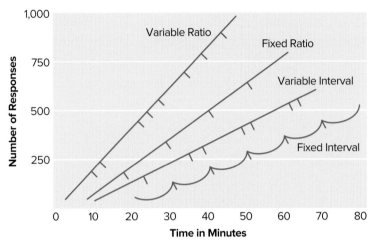

FIGURE 51.1 Reinforcement schedules for operant conditioning

Operant conditioning fell out of favor

In the 1960s and 1970s operant conditioning was *the* theory at many university psychology departments around the world. But many psychologists from other points of view (for example, cognitive or social psychology) were not fans, and it fell out of favor after that. Other learning and motivation theories became more popular, and these days operant conditioning gets maybe one lecture and a few pages in the textbook during a college Introductory Psychology class. If you haven't guessed, I was trained in operant conditioning during my undergraduate work, and I'm a fan. Although I do not believe that operant conditioning explains all behavior and motivation, I do believe that the theories are well tested, and they work. I've personally used them in my management style, my classroom style when I'm teaching, and in my child-rearing practices.

You can predict, then, how often people will engage in a certain behavior based on the way they are reinforced or rewarded. If you want someone to engage in a certain behavior the most, then you would use a variable ratio schedule.

If you've ever been to Las Vegas, then chances are you've seen a variable ratio schedule in operation. You put your money in the slot machine and press the button. You don't know how often you'll win. It's not based on time, but rather on the number of times you play. And it's not a fixed schedule, but a variable one. It's not predictable. You're not sure when you're going to win, but you know that your odds of winning increase the more times you play. So it will result in you playing the most, and the casino making the most money.

OPERANT THEORY AND DESIGN

If you're not sure that operant conditioning is related to design, think about it more deeply. Many times as designers you want to encourage people to engage in a certain behavior continuously. Skinner's work is still relevant, but people don't realize it. Take the study by Kivetz in the beginning of this chapter. The rewards card is actually an example of a fixed ratio schedule: you buy 10 cups of coffee (press the bar 10 times), and then you get a free coffee.

At Dropbox.com, for every friend you get to join Dropbox you receive extra storage space (**Figure 51.2**). This is called a continuous reinforcement schedule. (Skinner's work suggests that Dropbox might get better results if it gave a larger reward for every three or five friends, in other words, if it switched to a fixed ratio schedule rather than a continuous schedule).

Invite your friends to Dropbox!
For every friend who joins Dropbox, we'll give you both 250 MB of bonus space (up to a limit of 8 GB)!

FIGURE 51.2 For every friend who joins Dropbox, you get a reward

Takeaways

✳ For operant conditioning to work, the reinforcement (reward) must be something that particular audience wants. Hungry rats want food pellets. What does your particular audience really want?

✳ Think about the pattern of behavior you're looking for, and then adjust the schedule of rewards to fit that schedule. Use a variable ratio schedule for the maximum behavior repetition.

52 DOPAMINE MAKES PEOPLE ADDICTED TO SEEKING INFORMATION

Do you ever feel like you're addicted to e-mail or Twitter or texting? Do you find it impossible to ignore your e-mail if you see that there are messages in your inbox? Have you ever gone to Google to look up some information and realized 30 minutes later that you've been reading and linking and searching around for something totally different than before? These are all examples of your dopamine system at work.

Neuroscientists have been studying what they call the dopamine system since 1958, when it was identified by Arvid Carlsson and Nils-Ake Hillarp at the National Heart Institute of Sweden. Dopamine is created in various parts of the brain and is critical in all sorts of brain functions, including thinking, moving, sleeping, mood, attention, motivation, seeking, and reward.

PLEASURE CHEMICAL OR MOTIVATION CHEMICAL?

You may have heard that dopamine controls the "pleasure" systems of the brain that make you feel enjoyment. But researchers have recently found that instead of causing you to experience pleasure, dopamine actually causes you to want, desire, seek out, and search. It increases your general level of arousal, motivation, and goal-directed behavior. It's not only about physical needs such as food or sex, but also about abstract concepts. Dopamine makes you curious about ideas and fuels your search for information. The latest research shows that it is the opioid system, more than the dopamine system, that is involved in feelings of pleasure.

According to Kent Berridge (1998), these two systems—the "wanting" (dopamine) and the "liking" (opioid)—are complementary. The wanting system propels you to action and the liking system makes you feel satisfied, and therefore makes you pause your seeking. If your seeking isn't turned off, then you start to run in an endless loop. The dopamine system is stronger than the opioid system. You seek more than you are satisfied.

 Dopamine evolved to keep us alive

Dopamine is critical from an evolutionary standpoint. If humans had not been driven by curiosity to seek out things and ideas, then they would have just sat in their caves. The dopamine seeking system kept our ancestors motivated to move through the world, learn, and survive. Seeking was more likely to keep them alive than sitting around in a satisfied stupor.

Anticipation is better than getting

Brain scan research shows that our brains show more stimulation and activity when we *anticipate* a reward than when we get one. Research on rats shows that if you destroy dopamine neurons, rats can walk, chew, and swallow, but they will starve to death even when food is right next to them. They have lost the desire to go get the food.

Takeaways

✳ People are motivated to keep seeking information.

✳ The easier you make it for people to find information, the more information-seeking behavior they will engage in.

53 UNPREDICTABILITY KEEPS PEOPLE SEARCHING

Dopamine is also stimulated by unpredictability. When something happens that is not exactly predictable, it stimulates the dopamine system. Think about electronic devices. E-mails and tweets and texts show up, but you don't know exactly when they will arrive, or who they will be from. It's unpredictable. This is exactly what stimulates the dopamine system. It's the same system at work for gambling and slot machines. Basically e-mail, Twitter, and most social media run on the variable ratio schedule discussed earlier in this chapter. That makes it likely that people will engage in the behavior again and again.

THE PAVLOVIAN REFLEX

The dopamine system is especially sensitive to cues that a reward is coming. If there is a small, specific cue that signifies that something is going to happen, that sets off your dopamine system. This is a Pavlovian response, named for the Russian scientist Ivan Pavlov who experimented with dogs. When dogs (and humans) see food, they begin to salivate. Pavlov paired food with a sound, for instance, a bell. The bell is a stimulus. Every time the dogs saw food they would also hear a bell, and they would salivate at the sight of the food. After a while the dogs would salivate at the sound of the bell. The food wasn't even necessary for salivation to occur. When a stimulus is paired with information-seeking behavior, such as a sound and a message when a text arrives on your phone (**Figure 53.1**) or sound or visual cue when an e-mail arrives in your inbox (**Figure 53.2**), you have the same Pavlovian response—dopamine is released and the information seeking starts all over again.

FIGURE 53.1 Getting a message that a text has come in is a Pavlovian cue

FIGURE 53.2 The visual cue of how many unopened messages are in your in-box keeps you in a dopamine loop

140 CHARACTERS IS EVEN MORE ADDICTIVE

The dopamine system is most powerfully stimulated when the information comes in small amounts, so that it doesn't full satisfy the desire for information. A short text or a tweet (which has a maximum of 140 characters) is ideally suited to sending the dopamine system raging (**Figure 53.3**).

FIGURE 53.3 Short and frequent, Twitter messages are ideal for stimulating the dopamine system

THE DOPAMINE LOOP

With the Internet, Twitter, and texting, you now have almost instant gratification of your desire to seek. Want to talk to someone right away? Send a text and they respond in a few seconds. Want to look up some information? Just type it into Google. Want to see what your friends are up to? Go to Twitter or Facebook. You can get into a dopamine-induced loop: dopamine starts you seeking, you get rewarded for seeking, and that makes you seek more. It becomes harder and harder to stop looking at email, stop texting, and stop checking your cell phone to see if you have a message or a new text.

 How to break dopamine loops

In contrast to wanting to set up dopamine loops, you might be tired of being in one yourself. The constant stimulation of the dopamine system can be exhausting. To break a dopamine loop you need to get away from the information-seeking environment, i.e., turn off your computer and leave your phone out of sight and reach. One of the most powerful things you can do to end a dopamine loop is to turn off the bells and rings and cues that tell you that a message or text has arrived.

Takeaways

＊ Pairing cues such as sounds with the arrival of information motivates people to seek more.

＊ Giving small bits of information and then providing a way for people to get more information results in more information-seeking behavior.

＊ The more unpredictable the arrival of information is, the more people will be addicted to seeking it.

54 PEOPLE ARE MORE MOTIVATED BY INTRINSIC REWARDS THAN EXTRINSIC REWARDS

Let's say you're an art teacher, and you want to encourage your class to spend more time drawing. You create a Good Drawing Certificate to give to your students. If your goal is to have them draw more and to stick with it, how should you give them the certificate? Should you give them one every time they draw? Or only sometimes?

Mark Lepper, David Greene, and Richard Nisbett (1973) conducted research on this question. They divided children into three groups:

★ Group 1 was the Expected group. The researchers showed the children the Good Drawing Certificate and asked if they wanted to draw in order to get the certificate.

★ Group 2 was the Unexpected group. The researchers asked the children if they wanted to draw, but didn't mention anything about a certificate. After the children spent time drawing, they received an unexpected drawing certificate.

★ Group 3 was the Control group. The researchers asked the children if they wanted to draw, but didn't mention a certificate and didn't give them one.

The real part of the experiment came two weeks later. During playtime the drawing tools were put out in the room. The children weren't asked anything about drawing; the tools were just put in the room and available. So what happened? Children in the Unexpected and Control groups spent the most time drawing. The children in Expected group, the ones who had received an expected reward, spent the least time drawing. *Contingent* rewards (rewards given based on specific behavior that is spelled out ahead of time) resulted in less of the desired behavior if the reward was not repeated. Later the researchers went on to do more studies like this, with adults as well as children, and found similar results.

 People are motivated unconsciously

You have the experience of deciding to achieve a particular goal, and so you think that motivation is a conscious process. But research by Ruud Custers and Henk Aarts (2010) shows that at least some goals occur unconsciously. Your unconscious sets the goal and then eventually the goal surfaces to conscious thought.

Promising monetary rewards releases dopamine

Brian Knutson (2001) found that when people are promised a monetary reward for work, there is increased activity in the nucleus accumbens—the same area that is active when people anticipate cocaine, tobacco, or any addictive substance. Dopamine is released, and there is an increase in risky behavior. Giving people money backfires, since they'll come to rely on the monetary reward and then are unwilling to work unless there is a monetary incentive.

FROM ALGORITHMIC WORK TO HEURISTIC WORK

In Drive (2009), Daniel Pink writes that until recently people did algorithmic work—follow a procedure to accomplish a task. But now 70 percent of people (in developing countries) do heuristic work—there are no set procedures. Traditional punishments and rewards are based on extrinsic motivation and work well for algorithmic work, not heuristic work. Heuristic work assumes the work itself provides intrinsic motivation through a sense of accomplishment.

 People are motivated by the possibility of being connected

In the "People Are Social Animals" chapter, I cover how social people are and how being social affects expectations and behaviors. The opportunity to be social is also a strong motivating factor. People will be motivated to use a product just because it allows them to connect with others.

Takeaways

✳ Don't assume that money or any other extrinsic reward is the best way to reward people. Look for intrinsic rewards rather than extrinsic rewards.

✳ If you're going to give an extrinsic reward, it will be more motivating if it is unexpected.

✳ If the product you're designing allows people to connect with other, people then they will be motivated to use it.

55 PEOPLE ARE MOTIVATED BY PROGRESS, MASTERY, AND CONTROL

Why do people donate their time and creative thought process to Wikipedia? Or the open source movement? When you stop and think about it, you realize that there are many activities that people engage in, even over a long period of time, that require high expertise, and yet offer no monetary or even career-building benefit. People like to feel that they are making progress. They like to feel that they are learning and mastering new knowledge and skills.

SMALL SIGNS OF PROGRESS CAN HAVE A BIG EFFECT

Because mastery is such a powerful motivator, even small signs of progress can have a large effect in motivating people to move forward to the next step in a task. At LinkedIn, they encourage you to finish filling in information on your profile by showing you how much information you have already answered (**Figure 55.1**).

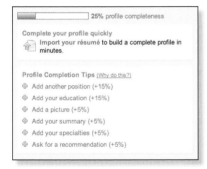

FIGURE 55.1 LinkedIn shows your progress in completing your profile

MailChimp shows you how many steps you have left to create an e-mail campaign (**Figure 55.2**).

Livemocha is a Web site where you can learn languages. The site has several forms of mastery and progress built in:

★ You can see at a glance where you are in the course, where you are in the lesson, and how much progress you have made overall (**Figure 55.3**).

FIGURE 55.2 MailChimp shows your progress in creating an e-mail campaign

FIGURE 55.3 Livemocha shows your progress at a glance
Courtesy of Livemocha (www.livemocha.com).

★ You can earn points by completing your training, as well as by helping other people learn a language you already know. The points can be accumulated and redeemed for access to premium learning exercises (**Figure 55.4**).

FIGURE 55.4 You can accumulate points at Livemocha by completing your lessons and helping others

Every time you sign on to Livemocha, you see a dashboard that shows your progress (**Figure 55.5**).

FIGURE 55.5 Livemocha shows you a dashboard as a way to motivate you to move forward

 Mastery can never actually be reached

In *Drive*, Daniel Pink says that mastery can be approached, but never really reached. **Figure 55.6** (on the next page) shows what this constant getting closer but never reaching looks like on a graph. The graph is known as an asymptote. You can get better and better, but you don't really reach an endpoint. This is one of the factors that makes mastery such a compelling motivator.

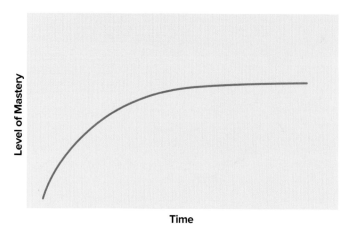

Level of Mastery

Time

FIGURE 55.6 According to Daniel Pink, mastery is an asymptote—it can never be fully reached

 Watch a video about Daniel Pink's ideas

Daniel Pink has a great animated video about the ideas in his book, *Drive*. You can watch the animated video at: http://www.youtube.com/watch?v=u6XAPnuFjJc

Takeaways

✳ If you want to build loyalty and have repeat customers (for example, repeat visitors to your Web site), you'll need to have activities that people inherently want to do (such as connecting with their friends, or mastering something new), rather than just activities for which people are getting paid.

✳ If people have to do a task that's boring, you can help motivate them by acknowledging that it's boring and then letting them do it their own way.

✳ Look for ways to help people set goals and track them.

✳ Show people how they're progressing toward goals.

56 PEOPLE'S ABILITY TO DELAY GRATIFICATION (OR NOT) STARTS YOUNG

You want to buy that Kindle, but you're thinking maybe you should wait a while. Maybe you should see if the price comes down later this year, or maybe you should pay down your credit card debt before you spend money on a new gadget for yourself. Do you wait or not?

Whether you're the type of person who can delay gratification or not, chances are high that you've been this way (a delayer or not a delayer) since you were a young child.

Starting in the late 1960s and early 1970s, Walter Mischel conducted a series of studies on delayed gratification. Years later he followed up with the original people in his study. He found that when the people in the study who were able to delay gratification became teenagers, they were more successful in school, received higher test scores on the SAT, and were better able to cope with stress and frustration. He followed them into adulthood and the differences continued. On the other side, the children in the original studies who could *not* delay gratification as preschoolers were more likely to have problems as adults, including drug abuse.

 Watch a video about Mischel's experiment

Here's a video with an update on Walter Mischel's experiment, called the Marshmallow Experiment: http://www.youtube.com/watch?v=6EjJsPylEOY

Ozlem Ayduk from the University of California, Berkeley, is bringing these same individuals back to the lab. The researchers are using fMRI brain imaging to get a better look at the parts of the brain that are active in delayed gratification. As I write this book, her research is not yet completed and published.

Takeaways

＊ Some people are good at delaying gratification and others are not.

＊ People who are not good at delaying gratification will be more suggestible to images and messages of scarcity (for example, "only three left in stock" or "only available till the end of the month").

57 PEOPLE ARE INHERENTLY LAZY

It might be exaggerating a bit to say that people are inherently lazy. But research does show us that people will do the least amount of work possible to get a task done.

IS LAZY ANOTHER WORD FOR EFFICIENT?

Over eons of evolution, humans have learned that they will survive longer and better if they conserve their energy. You want to spend enough energy to have enough resources (food, water, sex, shelter), but beyond that you are wasting your energy if you spend too much time running around getting or doing more stuff. Of course, questions about how much is enough, and whether we have enough stuff yet, and how long should the stuff last (and on and on), still vex us, but putting the philosophical questions aside, for most activities, most of the time, humans work on a principle called *satisficing*.

SATISFY PLUS SUFFICE EQUALS SATISFICE

Herbert Simon is credited with coining the term *satisfice*. He used it to describe a decision-making strategy in which the person decides to pick the option that is adequate, rather than optimal. The idea of satisficing is that the cost of making a complete analysis of all the options is not only not worth it, but may be impossible. According to Simon we often don't have the cognitive faculties to weigh all the options. So it makes more sense to make a decision based on "what will do" or what is "good enough" rather than trying to find the optimal or perfect solution. If people satisfice rather than optimize, there are implications for the design of Web sites, software, and other products.

DESIGN WEB SITES FOR SCANNING, NOT READING

In his book *Don't Make Me Think* (2005), Steve Krug applies the idea of satisficing to the behavior you can observe when someone comes to your Web site. You're hoping the visitor will read the whole page, but, as Krug says, "What they actually do most of the time (if we're lucky) is *glance* at each new page, scan *some* of the text, and click on the first link that catches their interest or vaguely resembles the thing they're looking for. There are usually large parts of the page that they don't even look at." Krug talks about Web pages being like billboards. You have to assume that people are taking a quick glance.

Keeping this idea in mind, look quickly at the following four screenshots of the home pages of several state government Web sites in the U.S. Imagine that you're making a trip to the state, and you're looking for tourism information. Don't study any of the pages, just glance briefly at **Figure 57.1**, **Figure 57.2**, **Figure 57.3**, and **Figure 57.4**.

FIGURE 57.1 Rhode Island state Web site

FIGURE 57.2 Mississippi state Web site

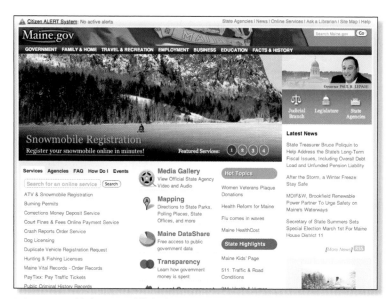

FIGURE 57.3 Maine state Web site

FIGURE 57.4 Texas state Web site

With this quick look you might get the feeling that the Maine and Texas Web sites will require less work than the others. You make a decision that a particular Web site will be easy to use based on the impression the site provides in one or two seconds of viewing. The Maine and Texas sites have more white space and a larger font size. Plus the Texas site puts Search literally front and center. These factors make it seem like it will be easy enough or good enough to find the information you're looking for. The first impressions about satisficing can be critically important in determining whether someone stays at the Web site or not.

Takeaways

* Assume that people will get things done with the least amount of work possible. That may not always be the case, but it's true more often than not.

* People will satisfice, that is, look for the good-enough solution rather than the optimal solution.

58 PEOPLE WILL LOOK FOR SHORTCUTS ONLY IF THE SHORTCUTS ARE EASY

Do you use keyboard shortcuts when you're typing on the computer? Do you use some, but not others? Why do you do that?

People will look for ways to do something faster and with fewer steps. This is especially true if it's a task they're doing over and over. But if the shortcut is too hard to find, or if a habit is ingrained, then people will keep doing it the old way. This seems paradoxical, but it's all about the perceived amount of work. If it seems like too much work to find a shortcut, then people will stay with their old habits (they are even satisficing about satisficing).

PROVIDE DEFAULTS

Defaults reduce the amount of work needed to complete a task. When you provide defaults, for example, filling in the person's name and address automatically on a Web form, then there is less work to finish the form. But there are some potential problems with defaults. One is that people don't always notice defaults, and so may end up accepting a default without meaning to. Here again, the answer lies in the amount of effort. If it takes a lot of work to change the result of accepting "wrong" defaults, then think twice about using them in your design.

When defaults create more work, not less

Recently I bought a pair of shoes online for my daughter. The next time I went to the Web site, it was to buy a pair of shoes for myself. But the default shipping address was the last address used—my daughter's, not mine. I didn't notice that the shipping address had filled in with a default that was not my home address. My daughter was surprised to get a pair of shoes she hadn't asked for. In this case, having a default operating meant a lot more work for both my daughter and me.

Takeaways

✳ Provide shortcuts as long as they are easy to learn, find, and use, but don't assume that people will always use them.

✳ Provide defaults if you know what most people will want to do most of the time, and if the result of choosing a default by mistake does not cause costly errors.

---

59 PEOPLE ASSUME IT'S YOU, NOT THE SITUATION

A man is walking down a busy city street on his way to an appointment, and he sees what looks like a college student drop a folder of papers. The papers scatter on the ground and the man glances over but keeps on walking. What do you think? Why didn't the man stop to help with the papers?

If you answer "Well, he's a self-absorbed person who doesn't usually help out strangers on the street," then chances are likely that you have just made a *fundamental attribution error.* People have a tendency to give personality-based explanations for other peoples' behavior more weight than situational factors. Alternatively, instead of explaining the person's behavior in the story above as being due to his "self absorption," you might ascribe his behavior to the situation, for example, "He's late for a critical meeting with the bank and doesn't have time to stop today. In other circumstances he would have stopped." But in reality you don't apply that situational motivation to him. You assume it's not the situation, but his personality that is causing his behavior.

BUT FOR YOU, IT'S SITUATIONAL

On the other hand, if you're analyzing and explaining your own behavior and motivations, then you will tend to think the opposite of what you attribute to others. In other words, you assume that your motivation and behavior are based on a reaction to the situation, not to personality factors. If you didn't stop and help the person pick up the papers, you would say it was because you were late for your meeting and didn't have time to stop, or some other situation-based explanation.

Research on the fundamental attribution error shows the following:

★ In cultures that value individualistic behavior (like the U.S.), it's common to ascribe other people's behavior to personality. The fundamental attribution error is common in these cultures.

★ On the other hand, in individualistic cultures people tend to ascribe their *own* behavior to situational factors more than personality factors.

★ In cultures that value collectivist behavior (China, for example), people make the same fundamental attribution error, but not as often as in individualist cultures.

Most of the research has to do with individuals deciding whether their actions are influenced by their personality versus situational factors. It seems that they are. People attribute the decisions of an "other group" to the individual member's attitudes, but attribute the decisions of their own group to the collective group rules.

PEOPLE CAN'T STOP IT EVEN WHEN THEY KNOW THEY'RE DOING IT

Research shows that it's very hard to stop making fundamental attribution errors. Even when you know you're doing it, and even if you know it's not accurate, you'll still make the same error.

 People are more willing to donate money to help victims of natural, as opposed to man-made, disasters

Hanna Zagefka (2010) asked people to read a fictitious news report about an island flooding disaster. One group of people read a report that implied that part of the reason for the flood was that the island's dams were not built effectively. A second group read a report that implied that the flood occurred because the storm was unusually strong, and didn't mention the dams being built incorrectly. Participants in the first group were less willing to donate money than those in the second group.

Similar results were found in another study about giving money to people affected by the 2004 tsunami versus the civil war in Darfur. If the researchers emphasized that the Darfur war was caused by ethnic conflict, then participants were less willing to donate because they saw it as caused by humans.

Zagefka performed additional research and always found the same result. If people thought the disaster was man-made, and that people could have done something differently, then participants were more willing to blame the people for the disaster.

Takeaways

✳ If you're interviewing people about how they would use the product you're designing, be careful of how you interpret or analyze the interviews. You'll have a tendency to think about "what people are going to do" based on personality and miss the situational factors.

✳ If you're interviewing a subject matter expert or domain expert who's telling you what people do or will do, think carefully about what you're hearing. The expert may miss situational factors and put too much value on people's personalities.

✳ Try to build in ways to cross-check your own biases. If your work requires you to make a lot of decisions about why people do what they do, you might want to stop before acting on your decisions and ask yourself, "Am I making a fundamental attribution error?"

60 FORMING A HABIT TAKES A LONG TIME AND REQUIRES SMALL STEPS

When you turn on your computer each morning, you first open your email, then you go on Facebook, then you go to weather.com to check the weather (or whatever your particular pattern is). You do this every day. It's a habit. Why are you motivated to do these same tasks every day? What did it take for these activities to become a habit? What would it take to change the habit to something else?

Philippa Lally (2010) recently studied the "how" and "how long" of forming habits. She had people choose an eating, drinking, or activity behavior to carry out every day for 12 weeks. In addition, the participants had to go online and complete a self-report habit index each day to record whether or not they had carried out the behavior.

HOW LONG IT TAKES TO CEMENT A HABIT

The average amount of time it took for people to form a habit was 66 days, but that number doesn't really tell the story, because there was a wide range. For some people and some behaviors it took 18 days, but depending on the person and the behavior, it went all the way up to 254 days for the behavior to become an automatic habit. This is a lot longer than has been written about before. Lally found that people would initially show an increase in the automaticity of the behavior, and then they would hit a plateau: their behavior followed an asymptote curve (**Figure 60.1**).

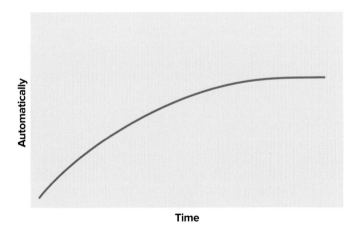

FIGURE 60.1 Creating a new habit forms an asymptote curve

SOME BEHAVIORS BECOME HABIT FASTER THAN OTHERS

The more complex the behavior, the longer it took to become a habit (no surprise there). Participants who chose to create an exercise habit took one-and-a-half times longer to make it automatic than those who were building a new habit about eating fruit at lunch.

HOW BAD IS IT TO MISS A DAY?

Lally found that if people missed a day here and there, it didn't have a significant effect on how long it took to build the habit. But too many missed days, or multiple days in a row, did have an effect, and slowed the creation of the habit. Not surprisingly, the more consistent people were, the more quickly they reached the automatic point, although missing one day did not delay habit formation. Missing two or more days did.

 Don't hesitate to forgive yourself

Michael Wohl (2010) found that the most effective way to prevent procrastination in the future is to forgive yourself now for the procrastinations you've done in the past.

 Motivate others to create a new habit by having them commit to something small

If you want people to commit to something big, you first need to get them to commit to something that is related, but very small. This changes their self-persona, which opens the door to larger commitments. When people form a habit, they are essentially making a new commitment. Choose something small for them to do first and then you can build a bigger habit and commitment later.

Takeaways

✳ Give people a small, easy task to do, rather than a complex one.

✳ Give people a reason to come back and do the task every day or almost every day.

✳ Be patient. Creating a habit may take a long time.

61 PEOPLE ARE MORE MOTIVATED TO COMPETE WHEN THERE ARE FEWER COMPETITORS

Did you take standardized tests like the SAT and ACT to get into college? How many people were in the room when you took the test? What does it matter? Research by Stephen Garcia and Avishalom Tor (2009) shows that it may matter a lot. Garcia and Tor first compared SAT scores for locations that had many people in the room taking the test versus locations that had smaller numbers. They adjusted the scores to control for the educational budget in that region and other factors. Students who took the SAT test in a room with fewer people scored higher. Garcia and Tor hypothesized that when there are only a few competitors, you (perhaps unconsciously) feel that you can come out on top, and so you try harder. And, the theory goes, when there are more people, it's harder to assess where you stand and therefore you're less motivated to try to come out on top. They called this the *N* effect, with *N* equaling number as in formulas.

COMPETING AGAINST 10 COMPETITORS VS. COMPETING AGAINST 100

Garcia and Tor decided to test their theory in the lab. They asked students to complete a short quiz, and told them to complete it as quickly and accurately as possible. They were told that the top 20 percent would receive $5. Group A was told that they were competing against 10 other students. Group B was told that they were competing against 100 other students. Participants in Group A completed the quiz significantly faster than those in Group B—Group A had greater motivation knowing they were competing against fewer people. The interesting thing is that there was no one actually in the room with them. They were just told that other people were taking the test.

Takeaways

✳ Competition can be motivating, but don't overdo it.

✳ Showing more than 10 competitors can dampen the motivation to compete.

---

62 PEOPLE ARE MOTIVATED BY AUTONOMY

How many times in a typical day or week do you go to a self-serve Web site or product—the ATM, the Web site to renew your driver's license, the online banking Web site, the online brokerage Website? How many products do you use that allow you to do things yourself rather than having to go through another person?

You've heard people complain about self-service ("What happened to the good old days when you could talk to an actual person?"), but people actually like to be independent, to feel that they're doing things on their own, with minimal help from others. People like to do things the way they want to do them, and when they want to do them. People like autonomy. Rather than hire an expert, people often want to do things on their own. An example is App Inventor from Google that helps people create their own apps (**Figure 62.1**).

App Inventor for Android
App Inventor is the easiest way to create apps for your phone! App Inventor is built on the idea that you do not need to be a developer to build great mobile applications. Instead of code, App Inventor allows you to visually design applications and use blocks to specify application logic.
December 15, 2010 ☆☆☆☆☆ 288 Ratings   Details and feedback »

FIGURE 62.1 App Inventor from Google allows people to do it themselves

 Autonomy motivates people because it makes them feel in control

The unconscious part of the brain likes to feel that it's in control. If you're in control, then there is less likelihood that you'll be in danger. The "old brain" is all about keeping you out of danger. Control equals keep out of danger equals do it yourself equals motivated by being autonomous.

Takeaways

✳ People like to do things themselves, and are motivated to do so.

✳ If you want to increase self-service, make sure your messaging is about having control and being able to do it yourself.

PEOPLE ARE SOCIAL ANIMALS

We underestimate how important it is for people to be social. People will use whatever is around them to be social, and that includes technology. This chapter looks at the science behind social interactions.

63 THE "STRONG TIE" GROUP SIZE LIMIT IS 150 PEOPLE

You have your Facebook friends and your LinkedIn connections. Maybe you have people you follow and who follow you on Twitter. Then there are the colleagues you work with, people you know from your community organizations like schools and churches, and your personal friends, and your family members. How many people are in your network overall?

DUNBAR'S NUMBER

Evolutionary anthropologists study social groups in animals. One question they have been trying to answer is whether there is a limit on how many individuals different species have in their social group. Robin Dunbar (1998) studied different species of animals. He wanted to know if there was a relationship between brain size (specifically the neocortex) and the number of stable relationships in social groups. He came up with a formula for calculating the limit for different groups. Anthropologists call this Dunbar's number for the species.

THE SOCIAL GROUP SIZE LIMIT FOR HUMANS

Based on his findings with animals, Dunbar then extrapolated what the number would be for humans. He calculated that 150 people is the social group size limit for humans. (To be more exact, he calculated the number at 148, but rounded up to 150. Also there is a fairly large error measure, so that the 95 percent confidence interval is from 100 to 230—for you statistical experts out there).

 Dunbar's number holds across time and cultures

Dunbar has documented the size of communities in different geographic areas and throughout different historical time frames, and he is convinced that this number holds true for humans across cultures, geographies, and time frames.

He assumes that the current size of the human neocortex showed up about 250,000 years ago, so he started his research with hunter-gatherer communities. He found that Neolithic farming villages averaged 150 people, as did Hutterite settlements, professional armies from the Roman days, and modern army units.

There's a limit to stable social relationships

The limit specifically refers to the number of people with whom you can maintain stable social relationships. These are relationships where you know who each person is and you know how each person relates to every other person in the group.

DOES THAT NUMBER SEEM LOW TO YOU?

When I talk about Dunbar's number of 150 for humans, most people think that is way too low. They have many more connections than that. Actually 150 is the group size for communities that have a high incentive to stay together. If the group has intense survival pressure, then it stays at the 150 member mark, and stays in close physical proximity. If the survival pressure is not intense, or the group is physically dispersed, then he estimates the number would be even lower. This means that, for most of us in our modern society, the number would not even be as high as 150. In the world of social media, people may have 750 Facebook friends, and 4,000 Twitter followers. A Dunbar's number advocate, however, would respond that these are not the strong, stable relationships that Dunbar is talking about, where everyone knows everyone and people are in close proximity.

IS IT THE WEAK TIES THAT ARE IMPORTANT?

Some critics of Dunbar's number say that what's really important in social media is not the strong ties that Dunbar talks about, but the weak ties—relationships that don't require everyone to know everyone else in the group, and which are not based on physical proximity. (Weak does not imply less important in this context.) Jacob Morgan, a social business advisor, argues that we find social media so interesting because they allow us to quickly and easily expand these "weak" ties, and that those ties are most relevant in our modern world.

 Learn more about the Dunbar and Morgan debate

First watch this interview with Robin Dunbar,
http://www.guardian.co.uk/technology/video/2010/mar/12/dunbar-evolution

And then read Jacob Morgan's blog post:
http://www.socialmediatoday.com/SMC/169132

✳ There is a limit of approximately 150 people for your "survival" community in close proximity. If you don't feel you have that "tribe" around you, you may feel alienated, isolated, and stressed.

✳ Your relationships with larger numbers of people through social media are likely weak ties.

✳ When you are designing a product that has social connections built in or implied, think about whether those interactions are for strong or weak ties.

✳ If you are designing for strong ties, you need to build in some amount of physical proximity, and make it possible for people to interact and know each other in the network.

✳ If you are designing for weak ties, don't rely on direct communication among all people in a person's network or physical proximity.

64 PEOPLE ARE HARD-WIRED FOR IMITATION AND EMPATHY

If you put your face right in front of a baby and stick out your tongue, the baby will stick out his or her tongue, too. This happens from a very young age, even as young as a month old. So what does this have to do with anything? It's an example of our built-in, wired-into-the-brain capacity for imitation. Recent research on the brain shows how our imitative behavior works; and in your design you can use this knowledge to influence behavior.

MIRROR NEURONS FIRING

The front of the brain contains an area called the premotor cortex (motor, as in movement). This is not the part of the brain that actually sends out the signals that make you move. *That* part of the brain is the primary motor cortex. The premotor cortex makes *plans* to move.

Let's say you're holding an ice cream cone. You notice that the ice cream is dripping, and you think that maybe you should lick off the dripping part before it drips on your shirt. If you were hooked up to an fMRI machine, you would first see the premotor cortex lighting up while you're thinking about licking off the dripping cone, and then you would see the primary motor cortex light as you move your arm. Now here comes the interesting part. Let's say it's not you that has the dripping ice cream cone. It's your friend. You are watching your friend's cone start to drip. If you watch your friend lift his arm and lick the dripping cone, a subset of the same neurons also fire in your premotor cortex. Just watching other people take an action causes some of the same neurons to fire as if you were actually taking the action yourself. This subset of neurons has been dubbed *mirror neurons*.

 Mirror neurons are the starting point of empathy

The latest theories are that mirror neurons are also the way we empathize with others. We are literally experiencing what others are experiencing through these mirror neurons, and that allows us to deeply, and literally, understand how another person feels.

Mimicking other people's body language makes them like you more

Watch two people talking. If you observe them closely, you will see that over time the two people start to imitate each other's body language. If one leans in, the other leans in. If one touches his face, the other person touches his face.

Tanya Chartrand and John Bargh (1999) had people sit down and talk with someone (a "confederate" who was actually part of the experiment, but the participants didn't know that). The confederates would vary their gestures and movements in a planned way. Some confederates were told to smile a lot, others to touch their faces, and others to jiggle their feet. The participants in the study would start to (unconsciously) imitate their confederates. Some behaviors increased more than others. Face touching increased by 20 percent but foot jiggling increased by 50 percent.

In another experiment Chartrand and Bargh had two groups. In one group, the confederate imitated the participant's movements, and in the second group the confederate did not imitate the participant. After the conversation, the participants were asked how much they liked the confederate, and how well they thought the interaction had gone. The group where the confederate had imitated the participant gave the confederate and the interaction overall higher ratings than the group where the confederate had not imitated the participant.

V. S. Ramachandran's research on mirror neurons

Vilayanur Ramachandran is one of the leading researchers on mirror neurons. I recommend that you watch a TED talk where he describes his research: http://bit.ly/aaiXba

Takeaways

✳ Don't underestimate the power of watching someone else do something. If you want to influence someone's behavior, then show someone else doing the same task.

✳ Research shows that stories create images in the mind that may also trigger mirror neurons. Use stories if you want to get people to take an action.

✳ Video at a Web site is especially compelling. Want people to get a flu shot? Then show a video of other people in line at a clinic getting a flu shot. Want kids to eat vegetables? Then show a video of other kids eating vegetables. Mirror neurons at work.

65 DOING THINGS TOGETHER BONDS PEOPLE TOGETHER

What do members of a marching band, fans cheering at a high school football game, and people at church have in common? They are all engaging in *synchronous activity*.

Anthropologists have long been interested in rituals among certain cultures, such as drumming, dancing, and singing. Scott Wiltermuth and Chip Heath (2009) conducted a series of studies to examine in more detail whether, and how, synchronous behavior affects how people cooperate. They tested combinations of walking in step, not walking in step, singing together, and other movements with groups of participants. What they found was that people who engaged in synchronous activities were more cooperative in completing subsequent tasks, and more willing to make personal sacrifices in order to benefit the group.

Synchronous activities are actions you take together with others, where everyone is doing the same thing at the same time in physical proximity to one another. Dancing, tai chi, yoga, singing, and chanting in time as a group are all examples of synchronous activity.

Wiltermuth and Heath's research also showed that you don't have to feel good about the group, or the group activity, in order to be more cooperative. Just the act of doing the synchronous activity seems to strengthen social attachment among the group members.

 Do people need synchronous activity to be happy?

In his article on "Hive Psychology, Happiness, and Public Policy," Jonathan Haidt (2008) connects synchronous activity and mirror neurons with anthropology and evolutionary psychology. Essentially his hypothesis is that synchronous activity promotes bonding and therefore helps the group survive. Mirror neurons are involved in synchronous activity, and there is a certain type of happiness that humans can't get any other way than engaging in synchronous activity.

Takeaways

* Many of our online interactions are asynchronous, including most social media (Twitter, Facebook, LinkedIn). Although asynchronous social activity fulfills other social needs, it does not fulfill our desire and pleasure from synchronous activity.

* Because most online interactions don't take place with others in physical proximity, there are limited opportunities for designers to build in synchronous activity.

* Look for opportunities to build synchronous activity into your product, using live video streaming, or a live video or audio connection.

66 PEOPLE EXPECT ONLINE INTERACTIONS TO FOLLOW SOCIAL RULES

There's a lot of discussion about social media, but what does the term *social media* really mean now? Many people think about social media as "social" software or applications that you use to market your business or organization or brand more effectively online. But if you stop to think about it, you'll realize that all online interactions are social interactions. Just the act of going to a Web site is a social interaction. Filling out a form at a government Web site to renew your automobile registration is a social interaction.

RULES FOR SOCIAL INTERACTIONS

When people interact with each other, they follow rules and guidelines for social interaction. Let's say you're sitting outside a café when your friend Mark comes in and sees you sitting by the window. Mark comes over to you and says, "Hi Richard, how are you doing today?" Mark expects you to interact with him, and he expects that interaction to follow a certain protocol. He expects you to look at him, in fact, to look him in the eye. If your previous interactions have been positive, then he expects you to smile a little bit. Next, you're supposed to respond to him by saying something like, "I'm fine. I'm sitting outside here to enjoy the beautiful weather." Where the conversation goes next depends on how well you know each other. If you're casual acquaintances, then he might wind down the conversation, "Well, enjoy it while you can. Bye!" If you're close friends, then he might pull up a chair and engage in a longer conversation.

You both have expectations of how the interaction will go, and if either of you violates the expectations, then you'll get uncomfortable. For example, what if Mark starts the conversation with "Hi, Richard, how are you today?" but you don't respond? What if you ignore him? Or you won't look at him? What if you answered, "My sister never liked the color blue" and stared into space? Or what if you responded with personal information that was a bit too personal? Any of these scenarios would make Mark uncomfortable. He would probably try to end the conversation as quickly as possible, and avoid interacting with you the next time the opportunity arose.

ONLINE INTERACTIONS HAVE THE SAME RULES

The same is true of online interactions. When you go to a Web site or use an online application, you have assumptions about how the site will respond to you and what the interaction will be like. And many of these expectations mirror the expectations that you have for person-to-person interactions. If the Web site is not responsive or takes too long to load, it's like the person you're speaking to is not looking at you, or is ignoring you. If the site asks for personal information too early in the interaction, that's like the other person getting too personal. If the Web site does not save your information from session to session, that's like the other person not recognizing you or remembering that you know each other.

Figure 66.1 is an example of a Web page that violates social rules. As I'm writing this book, Barack Obama is the president of the United States. Let's say you want information on how President Obama is using social media to get people to be active in supporting his ideas. You search for and go to the Organizing for America Web site from the Democratic National Committee. The home page asks for your e-mail address and zip code before you can get into the site. (There is a button below to skip this, but the effect has already been established before you see the button).

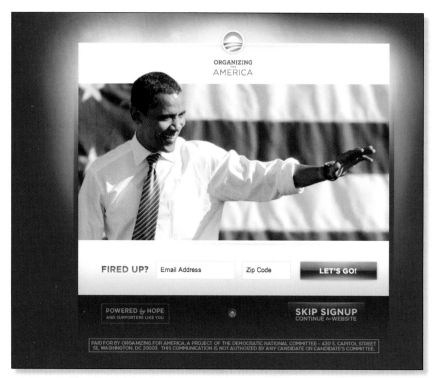

FIGURE 66.1 The Organizing for America Web site doesn't follow rules of social interaction

Here's what the Web page interaction is like from a social rule expectation viewpoint:

You're walking on the street and someone comes up to you and says, "Would you like to learn more about how you can support President Obama's policies?" The person is holding out a brochure to you. "Sure," you answer, and you go to take the brochure from the person's hand. He pulls the brochure away and says, "Oh, sorry. Before I can talk to you any further, or let you have this brochure, you have to give me your email address and your zip code." "Forget it," you respond and walk away. "Wait," he yells, "that's OK, we can skip the email address and zip code." But by now you don't trust him and don't want to interact.

Takeaways

* When you're designing a product think, about the interactions that the person will have with it. Do the interactions follow the rules of a person-to-person interaction?

* Many usability design guidelines for products are actually guidelines that connect to social expectations for interactions. Follow basic usability guidelines and you'll be more assured of meeting interactive expectations.

67 PEOPLE LIE TO DIFFERING DEGREES DEPENDING ON THE MEDIA

There are many ways to communicate: paper and pen, e-mail, face-to-face meetings, telephone, instant messaging. Some researchers have been interested in whether there are differences in how honest we are based on the medium.

NINETY-TWO PERCENT OF GRADUATE STUDENTS LIED

Charles Naquin (2010) from DePaul University and his colleagues have conducted research on honesty in people when using email versus pen and paper.

In one study, forty-eight graduate business students were each given $89 (imaginary money) to divide with their partner; they had to decide whether to tell their partner how much money was in the kitty, as well as how much of the money to share with their partner. One group communicated by email and the other group by a handwritten note. The group that wrote emails lied about the amount of money (92 percent) more than the group that was writing by hand (63 percent). The e-mail group was also less fair about sharing the money, and felt justified in not being honest or fair.

MANAGERS LIE, TOO

Lest you think only the students would lie, Naquin and team performed additional studies with managers. One hundred and seventy-seven managers played a group financial game. Participants were assigned to teams of three. Each member of the team had a chance to play the role of a manager of a project team who was allocating money for projects. They played with real money, and they were told that the amount of money available would be revealed after the game. Some participants were told to communicate via e-mail and others with paper and pen. The managers who communicated via e-mail lied more, and kept more money for themselves, compared to the managers who communicated with paper and pen.

 Harsher ratings on performance reviews

Terri Kurtzberg (2005) and her team did three studies to see whether people gave different performance review ratings if the reviews were done via e-mail versus with pen and paper. In all three studies participants gave more negative appraisals of their peers when communicating via e-mail than when using pen and paper.

PEOPLE LIE MOST ON THE TELEPHONE

At this point you might be thinking that e-mails are the worst in terms of lying. They're not. Jeff Hancock (2004) conducted a diary study. Using self-reporting, participants admitted to lying most on the phone, and least in email, with face-to-face and instant messaging interactions equal and in the middle of the other techniques.

The moral disengagement theory

Albert Bandura, a social psychologist from Stanford University, hypothesized that people can and will become unethical as they distance themselves from the bad consequences of their actions. He called this the moral disengagement theory (Bandura, 1999). In discussing the results of his studies about email, Charles Naquin (2010) and his team suggests that e-mail causes that distancing because it is viewed as less permanent, and because people feel less trust and rapport online.

How to tell who is lying in an e-mail

Jeff Hancock (2008) reports that liars write more words (28 percent more) than people who are telling the truth, and that liars use less first-person references (I, me) and more second and third-person references (you, he, she, they). Interestingly, most people in the research were not very good at figuring out when they were being lied to.

Takeaways

* People lie most on the phone, and least with pen and paper.

* People are more negative toward others via e-mail than with pen and paper.

* If you're designing surveys via e-mail, realize that people are likely to be more negative than they would be using pen and paper.

* If you are conducting a survey or getting audience feedback, be aware that telephone surveys will not get you as accurate a response as email or pen and paper surveys will.

* Getting customer or audience feedback is most accurate when done in person, one-on-one.

68 SPEAKERS' BRAINS AND LISTENERS' BRAINS SYNC UP DURING COMMUNICATION

When you listen to someone talking, your brain starts working in sync with the speaker. Greg Stephens (2010) and his team put participants in his research study in an fMRI machine and had them record or listen to recordings of other people talking. He found that as people listen to someone else talk, the brain patterns of both speaker and listener start to couple, or mirror each other. There's a slight delay, which corresponds to the time it takes for the communication to occur. Several different brain areas were synced. He compared this with having people listen to someone talk in a language they did not understand. In that case the brains do not sync up.

SYNCING PLUS ANTICIPATION EQUALS UNDERSTANDING

In Stephens's study, the more the brains were synced up, the more the listener understood the ideas and message from the speaker. And by watching what parts of the brain were lighting up, Stephens could see that the parts of the brain that have to do with prediction and anticipation were active. The more active they were, the more successful the communication was. Stephens noted that the parts of the brain that have to do with social interaction were also synced, including areas known to be involved in processing social information crucial for successful communication, such as the capacity to discern the beliefs, desires, and goals of others. Stephens also hypothesizes that mirror neurons are involved in the speaker-listener brain syncing.

Takeaways

* Listening to someone talk creates a special brain syncing that helps people understand what is being said.

* Presenting information through audio and/or video where people can hear someone talking is an especially powerful way to help people understand the message.

* Don't just rely on reading if you want people to understand information clearly.

69 THE BRAIN RESPONDS UNIQUELY TO PEOPLE YOU KNOW PERSONALLY

Your Uncle Arden invites you over to watch the World Cup and tells you to bring some friends. When you get there, you see that there are several people you know (relatives and friends of relatives), and some you don't know. It's a lively bunch, and over food and the game on TV, lots of topics are covered, including soccer and politics. As you would expect, you have similar opinions as some of your friends and relatives, and you disagree with some of them. You actually have more in common, in terms of soccer and politics, with some of the strangers you just met today than you have with some of your friends and relatives. When it comes to the people in the room, you have essentially four possible connections as shown in **Figure 69.1**.

Similar	Friends and relatives that I have a lot in common with	Strangers that I have a lot in common with
Not Similar	Friends and relatives that I don't have a lot in common with	Strangers that I don't have a lot in common with

FIGURE 69.1 The four possible connections with the people at the World Cup party

The question that Fenna Krienen (2010) conducted research on is this: Does your brain react differently to these four combinations? Do you make judgments about other people based on how similar they are to you? Or is it more important that they be close to you, either a close friend or a relative? And if there are differences, will they show up on fMRI brain scans? When you think about people that you don't know, but feel similar to, do the same brain regions light up as though you were connected to them through kinship or previous friendship?

Krienen and her team tested these theories. They found that when people answered questions about friends, whether or not they felt they were similar to their friends, the medial prefrontal cortex (MPFC) was active. The MPFC is the part of the brain that perceives value and regulates social behavior. When people thought about others that they don't know, but had common interests with, the MPFC was not active.

 Facebook vs. Twitter and the MPFC

Jonah Lehrer (2010) writes about the difference between Facebook and Twitter. He says that Facebook is your friends and relatives that you know well, even if you aren't similar in how you think about everything. Facebook activates the MPFC. Twitter is more about helping you connect to people that you don't already know.

Takeaways

✳ All social media are not alike. It may be important to distinguish between social media for friends and relatives versus social media for people you're not already connected to.

✳ People are "programmed" to pay special attention to friends and relatives. Social media around friends and relatives will be more motivating and garner more loyalty. You're more likely to check your Facebook page five times a day than your LinkedIn page, because the former is about friends and relatives.

70 LAUGHTER BONDS PEOPLE TOGETHER

How many times a day do you hear someone laugh? Laughter is so ubiquitous that you don't even stop to think about what it is and why people do it.

There's less research on laughter than you might think. But a few people have spent time researching it. Robert Provine is one of the few neuroscientists studying laughter. He has concluded that laughter is an instinctual (not learned) behavior that creates social bonding.

Provine (2001) has spent many hours observing when and why people laugh. He and his team observed 1,200 people spontaneously laughing in different locations. They took notes on gender, situation, speaker, listener, and context. Here's a summary of what they found:

★ Laughter is universal. All humans in all cultures laugh.

★ Laughter is unconscious. People can't actually laugh on command—it will be fake laughter if they try.

★ Laughter is for social communication. People rarely laugh when they're alone. They laugh 30 times more often when they're with others.

★ Laughter is contagious. People will smile and then start laughing as they hear others laugh.

★ Laughter appears early in babies at about four months old.

★ Laughter isn't about humor. Provine studied over 2,000 cases of naturally occurring laughter and most of it did not happen as a result of humor such as telling jokes. Most laughter followed statements such as "Hey John, where ya been?" or "Here comes Mary" or "How did you do on the test?" Laughter after these types of statements bonds people together socially. Only 20 percent of laughter is from jokes.

★ People rarely laugh in the middle of a sentence. It's usually at the end.

★ The person who is speaking laughs twice as much as the person who is listening.

★ Women laugh more than twice as much as men.

★ Laughter denotes social status. The higher up on the hierarchy you are in a group, the *less* you will laugh.

TICKLE LAUGHTER VERSUS JOY LAUGHTER

Diana Szameitat (2010) and her team studied laughter produced from tickling versus laughter from other sources. They had people listen to recordings of people laughing while being tickled versus laughing without tickling. When people listened to regular laughter without tickling, they showed activity in the medial frontal cortex of the brain. This is a region that is usually associated with social and emotional processing. When people listened to laughter during tickling, they showed activity in the same region, but also activity in the secondary auditory cortex. Tickle laughter sounds different.

The researchers think that laughter might have started in animals as a reflex-like reaction to touch, and then became differentiated over time through various animals and species.

 Other animals laugh, too

It's not just a people thing. Chimps tickle each other and even laugh when another chimp pretends to tickle them. Jaak Panksepp studies rats that laugh when he tickles them. You can watch a video on YouTube showing Panksepp tickling rats: http://bit.ly/gBYCKt

Takeaways

* Most online interactions are asynchronous and therefore don't afford a lot of opportunity for social bonding through laughing.

* Synchronous communication online should lead to more bonding if it allows for laughter.

* You don't necessarily need humor or jokes to get people to laugh. Normal conversation and interactions will produce more laughter than intentional use of humor or jokes.

* If you want people to laugh, then laugh yourself. Laughter is contagious.

71 PEOPLE CAN TELL WHEN A SMILE IS REAL OR FAKE MORE ACCURATELY WITH VIDEO

Research on smiling started as far back as the mid-1800s. A French doctor named Guillaume Duchenne used electrical currents with research subjects. He would stimulate certain facial muscles and then take pictures of the expressions that people made (**Figure 71.1**). This was painful and many of the pictures look like the people are in pain.

FIGURE 71.1 Guillaume Duchenne took photos of people whose facial muscles were electrically stimulated

REAL OR FAKE?

Duchenne identified two different types of smiles. Some smiles involve contraction of both the zygomatic major muscle (which raises the corners of the mouth) and the orbicularis oculi muscle (which raises the cheeks and makes the eyes crinkle). Smiles that contract both of these muscle groups are called Duchenne smiles. In a non-Duchenne smile only the zygomatic major muscle contracts; in other words, the mouth turns up, but the eyes don't crinkle.

After Duchenne, several researchers used these ideas to research smiling. For years it was believed that Duchenne smiles were the ones that were seen as genuine, that it was not possible to "fake" a smile, because up to 80 percent of people can't consciously control the muscles around the eyes that make them crinkle. Why all the interest in whether a smile is real or fake? Because people are quicker to trust and like other people who are showing what are believed to be genuine emotions rather than fake or contrived ones.

QUESTIONING THE 80 PERCENT FIGURE

Eva Krumhuber and Antony Manstead (2009) decided to research whether it was true that most people couldn't create a fake smile that looks real. They found the opposite of what was previously believed. In their research, when photos were taken of people pretending to smile, 83 percent of the people could produce fake smiles that other people thought were real.

They also decided to test videos rather than just photos. What they found was that it was harder to fake a smile in a video, but not because of the crinkly eyes. People could tell real from fake by paying attention to other factors, such as how long they held the smile, and whether they saw other emotions besides happiness, for example, a flicker of impatience. The video made it easier to detect a fake smile because it lasted longer and was dynamic, instead of just a snapshot.

Takeaways

＊ Pay attention to smiles in videos. People will be able to determine a fake smile versus a real one better in a video than in a photo. If they don't think the smile is real, they're less likely to trust you.

＊ It is possible to fake a smile and to fake a crinkly-eye smile, but it is easier to fake a smile in a static picture than on a video.

＊ People can tell whether a smile is real or not by looking for conflicting emotions. They are looking at many parts of the face, not just the eyes.

＊ If a smile looks real, it will engage the viewer and build trust.

HOW
PEOPLE
FEEL

People don't just think. They also feel. In addition to understanding your audience's demographics, you need to also understand their psychographics.

72 SEVEN BASIC EMOTIONS ARE UNIVERSAL

Considering how important emotions are in our everyday life, there's not as much research on them as you might think. Scientists studying emotions distinguish them from moods and attitudes:

★ Emotions have physiological correlates, are expressed physically (through gestures, facial expressions, and so on), result from a specific event, and often lead to an action.

★ Moods last longer than emotions, perhaps a day or two. They may not be expressed physically, and may not come from a specific event.

★ Attitudes have a more cognitive, conscious brain component.

★ Joseph LeDoux (2000) has shown that certain parts of the brain activate when people are feeling certain emotions.

FACIAL EXPRESSIONS ARE UNIVERSAL; GESTURES ARE NOT

Paul Ekman is the expert in reading emotions in facial expressions. He has written two books, *Emotions Revealed: Recognizing Faces and Feelings to Improve Communication and Emotional Life* (2007), and *Telling Lies: Clues to Deceit in the Marketplace, Politics, and Marriage* (2009), and is a consultant to the Fox TV series *Lie to Me.* He has identified seven emotions that seem to be universal (**Figure 72.1**): joy, sadness, contempt, fear, disgust, surprise, and anger.

According to Ekman's work, 40 facial muscles comprise the main muscles used in showing emotion. You can take a one-hour online course at http://face.paulekman.com/default.aspx to learn how to read "microexpressions" that tell what people are feeling. Several different research teams around the world are working on software to automate the reading of facial expressions.

Facial expressions seem to be universal, as are many vocalizations used to express emotions, such as crying and laughing (Disa Sauter, 2010). Gestures accompanying emotions are not as universal.

Joy   Sadnesss   Contempt   Fear

Disgust   Surprise   Anger

FIGURE 72.1 Paul Ekman's seven universal emotions

Takeaways

✳ The seven basic emotions of joy, sadness, contempt, fear, disgust, surprise, and anger are universal and are shown by facial expression and physical gestures.

✳ If you're using pictures to communicate (for example, pictures of people at a Web site), use one of the seven basic emotions in the picture to communicate them most clearly.

✳ People read the seven basic emotions fairly well from photos. Try to use photos where the expressions look real, as people can often detect fake emotions.

✳ Decide which emotions drive your target audience. In addition to basic demographic information, identify and document psychographics; for example, what emotions are motivating or will motivate different parts of your target audience?

73 EMOTIONS ARE TIED TO MUSCLE MOVEMENT AND VICE VERSA

Botox is a popular cosmetic product used to reduce facial wrinkles. It's injected into various muscles (for instance, in the face) and paralyzes them, thereby causing the wrinkles to relax. It's been known for some time that a side effect of Botox treatments is that people can't fully express emotions (for example, they can't move the muscles that show they're angry or even happy). New research shows that another side effect of the injections is that people can't *feel* emotions as well, either. If you can't move your muscles to make a facial expression, you can't feel the emotion that goes with the expression. So if you've recently received a Botox injection and you go to a movie that is sad, you won't feel sad because you won't be able to move the muscles in your face that go with feeling sad. Moving muscles and feeling emotions are linked.

Joshua Davis (2010) from Barnard College and his team tested this idea with some research. They injected people with either Botox or Restylane. Restylane is a substance that, when injected, fills out sagging skin, but does not limit muscle movement like Botox does. Before and after injecting the participants, they showed them emotionally charged videos. The Botox group showed much less emotional reaction to the videos after the injections.

David Havas (2010) gave people instructions to contract the specific muscles used in smiling. When the participants contracted those muscles, they had a hard time generating a feeling of anger. When he instructed them to contract the muscles that are used to frown, the participants had a hard time feeling friendly or happy.

 The brain mirrors emotions, too

When you observe someone who is feeling a certain emotion, the same parts of your brain are active as in the brain of the person experiencing the emotion. An example is the research of Nicola Canessa and her team (2009), who found that fMRI scans show this effect with the emotion of regret. Participants watched someone perform a gambling task. When the person doing the gambling made a decision that caused them to lose money, they felt regret, and certain parts of their brain were active during that feeling. When participants in the study watched people doing the gambling task, the same regions in the brain were activated.

Takeaways

✳ You may need to consider the emotions you're generating as people interact with your product. For example, if someone reads a sad story and is frowning, this may put them in a sad mood that might affect the next action they take.

✳ Watch out for unintended facial expressions that may change how people feel about your product. For example, if the font at your Web site is very small, and people are squinting and frowning to read it, that may actually prevent them from feeling happy or friendly, and that may affect an action you want them to take.

✳ This is another instance of the power of video. Because people mimic others' expressions (see #64 on mirror neurons), showing a video of someone who is happy and smiling will tend to make the person watching smile, which will then make them feel happy, and that in turn may change the next action they take.

74 ANECDOTES PERSUADE MORE THAN DATA

In my book *Neuro Web Design: What Makes Them Click?* I explain that most mental processing occurs unconsciously. People are unaware of this unconscious processing, so it's easy to give more weight to information that we're consciously aware of. It's easy to forget that information is coming in and being processed from many sources. It's easy to forget that you are processing emotions, too.

Let's say you have to make a presentation to the department heads at work about your latest conversations with your customers. You interviewed 25 customers and surveyed another 100, and have lots of important data to share. Your first thought might be to present a summary of the data in a numerical/statistical/data driven format, for example:

★ 75 percent of the customers we interviewed…

★ Only 15 percent of the customers responding to the survey indicated…

But this data-based approach will be less persuasive than anecdotes. You may want to include the data, but your presentation will be more powerful if you focus on one or more anecdotes, for example, "Mary M. from San Francisco shared the following story about how she uses our product…," and then go on to tell Mary's story.

One of the reasons why anecdotes are more powerful than data is that anecdotes are in story form. They invoke empathy, which triggers an emotional reaction. With emotional reactions, people will process the data and the feelings. Emotions will also trigger the memory centers.

Better yet, don't just tell Mary's story in the presentation—include a video of Mary telling the story herself. That makes an even more powerful emotional connection. (See the "People Are Social Animals" chapter for more information on why video is a powerful medium.)

Takeaways

✳ Information is processed more deeply and remembered longer if it has an emotional hook.

✳ Look for ways to provide a message that will invoke emotions and empathy.

✳ Use anecdotes in addition to, or in place of, factual data.

75 SMELLS EVOKE EMOTIONS AND MEMORIES

Do you have a type of food that evokes an emotional reaction when you smell it? For me it's kasha. Kasha is a form of buckwheat. The buckwheat kernels come roasted, and you cook them in oil and then boil them with salt, pepper, onion, and garlic. I've met very few people who have actually eaten kasha, much less know what kasha is.

When I smell kasha cooking, I get a big smile on my face and I feel happy. This is because my mother used to cook kasha. I have a positive emotional memory of her when I smell kasha cooking.

THE SPECIAL OLFACTORY PATH

The thalamus is the part of the brain between the cerebral cortex and the midbrain. One of its functions is to process sensory information and send it to the appropriate part of the cortex. For example, visual information comes from the retina, goes to the thalamus, and then gets routed to the primary visual cortex. All of the senses send their data to the thalamus before the information goes anywhere else, with the exception of smell. The olfactory system does not go through the thalamus. When you smell something, that sensory data goes right to your amygdala, where emotional information is processed. This is why people react emotionally to smells. You smell a flower and it makes you happy. You smell rotten meat and it makes you feel disgusted. The amygdala is right next to the memory centers of the brain. This is also why smelling something invokes memories.

 Companies are using scent for branding

Nearly two dozen companies specialize in scent branding—creating unique scents for particular brands to invoke particular feelings and emotions. The industry is estimated to have annual revenues of $80 million. Scenting machines are used in numerous hotels: Sheraton uses Welcoming Warmth, a mix of fig, jasmine, and freesia; Westin uses White Tea; Marriott uses Meeting Sense in its conference rooms (the "tangy effervescent zest" of orange blossom in the mornings and "an infusion of Mediterranean citrus, fruit, and herbs" in the afternoon). Retail stores including Sony, Samsung, and Abercrombie & Fitch, as well as casinos also use them. The cost to rent a scenting machine ranges from $100 to $10,000 a month depending on the size of the space to be scented.

You can even study scent as part of a master's program at the Parsons New School for Design in New York (http://www.newschool.edu/parsons/mfa-transdiciplinary-design/).

✳ Scents are used in retail stores, hotels, malls, and other places to evoke particular memories, emotions, and associations.

✳ Scents have been experimented with in movie theaters, and there is some research on using scents while people are learning information online with a computer.

✳ In the future, designing scents for emotional influence with be part of some user experience designers' skill sets.

76 PEOPLE ARE PROGRAMMED TO ENJOY SURPRISES

In *Neuro Web Design: What Makes Them Click?* I talk about the role of the "old brain" in scanning the environment for anything that could be dangerous. This also means that the unconscious, old brain is looking for anything new or novel.

CRAVING THE UNEXPECTED

Research by Gregory Berns (2001) shows that the human brain not only looks for the unexpected, it actually craves the unexpected.

Berns used a computer-controlled device to squirt either water or fruit juice into people's mouths while their brains were being scanned by an fMRI device. Sometimes the participants could predict when they were going to get a squirt, but other times it was unpredictable. The researchers thought that they would see activity based on what people liked. For example, if a participant liked juice then there would be activity in the nucleus accumbens, the part of the brain that is active when people experience pleasurable events.

However, that's not what happened. The nucleus accumbens was most active when the squirt was unexpected. It was the surprise that showed activity, not the preferred liquid.

 Nice surprises versus unpleasant surprises

Not all surprises are equal. If, when you come home and turn on the light, your friends yell "Surprise!" because it's your surprise birthday party, that's a very different kind of surprise than finding a burglar in your home.

Marina Belova and her team (2007) researched whether the brain processes these two different kinds of surprises in different locations.

The researchers worked with monkeys and the amygdala, a part of the brain where emotions are processed. In their research they recorded the electrical activity of neurons in the amygdala. They used a drink of water (pleasant) versus a puff of air to the face (which the monkeys do not like).

They found that some neurons responded to the water and others to the puff of air, but a specific neuron did not respond to both.

Takeaways

* Things that are new and novel capture attention.

* Providing something unexpected not only gets attention, but also can be actually pleasurable.

* Although a certain amount of consistency (at a Web site, for example) is a good thing if people are trying to complete a task, providing novel and unexpected content and interactions is good if you want people to try something new, or if you want them to come back to see what's new.

77 PEOPLE ARE HAPPIER WHEN THEY'RE BUSY

Consider this scenario: You've just landed at an airport and you have to walk to the baggage claim to pick up your luggage. It takes you 12 minutes to walk there. When you arrive your luggage is coming onto the carousel. How impatient do you feel?

Contrast that with this scenario: You've just landed at an airport, and the walk to the luggage carousel takes 2 minutes. Then you stand around waiting 10 minutes for your luggage to appear. How impatient do you feel now?

In both cases it took you 12 minutes to pick up your luggage, but chances are you are much more impatient, and much unhappier, in the second scenario where you have to stand around and wait.

PEOPLE NEED AN EXCUSE

Research by Christopher Hsee (2010) and his colleagues shows that people are happier when they're busy. This is somewhat of a paradox. In the "What Motivates People" chapter, I wrote that we are lazy. Unless people have a reason for being active, they'll choose to do nothing, thereby conserving energy. However, doing nothing makes people impatient and unhappy.

Hsee's team gave participants a choice between delivering a completed questionnaire to a location that was a 15-minute, round-trip walk away, or delivering it just outside the room and then waiting 15 minutes. Some participants were offered the same snack bar regardless of which activity they chose, and others were offered a different type of snack bar for the two options. (Hsee previously determined that both snack bars were considered equally desirable.)

If the same snack bar was offered at both locations, then most (68 percent) of the participants chose to deliver the questionnaire just outside the room (the "lazy" option). The students' first reaction was to do less work, but when they were given an excuse for walking further, most of them took the busy option. After the experiment, the students who'd taken the walk reported feeling significantly happier than the idle students. In a second version of the study, the students were assigned to either the "busy" or the "idle" option (in other words, they did not choose). The busier students, again, reported higher happiness scores.

In the next round of research, Hsee asked students to study a bracelet. Then he gave them the option of either spending 15 minutes waiting with nothing to do (they thought they were waiting for the next part of the experiment), or spending the same time taking the bracelet apart and then rebuilding it while waiting. Some of the participants were given the option of rebuilding it into its original configuration, and others were given the option to reassemble the bracelet into a different design.

Participants who had the option of rebuilding the bracelet as it was before preferred to just sit idly. But the participants who were told they could reassemble the bracelet into a new design preferred to work on the bracelet rather than sit idle. As before, those who spent the 15 minutes busy with the bracelet reported feeling happier than those who sat idle.

Takeaways

✳ People don't like to be idle.

✳ People will do a task rather than be idle, but the task has to be seen as worthwhile. If people perceive it to be busywork, then they prefer to stay idle.

✳ People who are busy are happier.

✳ If you have a task that requires people to wait, you'd better have something interesting for them to do while waiting.

78 PASTORAL SCENES MAKE PEOPLE HAPPY

Walk into any hotel, house, office building, museum, art gallery, or other place where there are paintings or photographs hanging on the wall, and chances are that you'll see a picture that looks something like **Figure 78.1**.

FIGURE 78.1 Pastoral scenes are part of our evolution. (*Evening at the River* by Stanislav Pobytov.)

According to Denis Dutton, a philosopher and the author of *The Art Instinct: Beauty, Pleasure, and Human Evolution,* you'll often see these types of images because we're drawn to them due to evolution during the Pleistocene era. (See Dutton's TED talk at http://bit.ly/clj9uo.) Dutton notes that typical landscape scenes include hills, water, trees (good for hiding in if a predator comes by), birds, animals, and a path moving through the scene. This is an ideal landscape for humans, containing protection, water, and food. Dutton's theory about beauty is that we have evolved to feel a need for certain types of beauty in our lives, and that this pull toward things such as these landscapes has helped us to survive as a species. He notes that all cultures value artwork that has these scenes, even people who have never lived in a geographical location that looks like this.

PASTORAL SCENES PROVIDE "ATTENTION RESTORATION"

Mark Berman (2008) and a team of researchers first had participants perform the *backward digit-span task,* which measures a person's capacity to focus attention. Next, participants were asked to do a task that would wear out their voluntary attention. After that, some participants were asked to walk through downtown Ann Arbor, Michigan, and some were asked to walk through the city's arboretum. The arboretum has trees and wide lawns (that is, it's a pastoral environment). Following the walk, the participants did the backward digit-span task again. Scores were higher for the people who had walked through the arboretum. Stephen Kaplan (one of the researchers) calls this Attention Restoration Therapy.

Roger Ulrich (1984) found that patients whose hospital window overlooked scenes of nature had shorter stays in the hospital, and needed less pain medication compared to patients whose rooms looked onto a brick wall.

Peter Kahn (2009) and his team, tested nature scenes in the workplace. One group of participants worked in an office where they sat near a glass window that overlooked a nature scene. A second group saw a similar scene, but not out the window; instead, they watched a video feed from a nature area outside. A third group sat near an empty wall. The researchers kept measurements of the participants' heart rates to monitor their stress levels.

People who saw the video scene said that they felt better, but their heart rates were actually no different from those who sat next to the wall. People in front of the glass window actually had healthier heart rate measurements, and were better able to recover from stress.

Takeaways

✳ People like pastoral scenes. If you're looking for a nature scene to use at a Web site, try to pick one with the pastoral elements.

✳ People will be drawn to, like, and feel happier looking at a pastoral scene online, but it won't have the same positive health effects as seeing the actual scene out a window or being able to walk through the pastoral setting.

79 PEOPLE USE LOOK AND FEEL AS THEIR FIRST INDICATOR OF TRUST

There isn't much actual research on trust and Web site design. There are many opinions, but not necessarily much real data. Research by Elizabeth Sillence (2004) and her team provides some solid data, at least in regard to health Web sites.

Sillence researched how people decide which health Web sites to trust and whether to trust them. Participants in the study were all patients with hypertension. (In previous research, Sillence used the topic of menopause and found similar results.) In this study participants used Web sites to look for information about hypertension.

When participants in the study rejected a health Web site as not being trustworthy, 83 percent of their comments were related to design factors, such as an unfavorable first impression of the look and feel, poor navigation, color, text size, or the name of the Web site.

When participants mentioned the features that were relevant to their decision that a Web site was trustworthy, 74 percent referenced the content of the site, rather than design factors. They preferred sites owned by well-known and respected organizations and those that had advice written by medical experts, with information that was specific to them, and that they felt was written for people like themselves.

 Trust is the biggest predictor of happiness

If you want to know who is happiest, then figure out who feels the most trust. In his book, *The Geography of Bliss* (2009), Eric Weiner travels the world investigating which countries have the happiest people and why. Here is some of what he discovered and writes about:

★ Extroverts are happier than introverts.

★ Optimists are happier than pessimists.

★ Married people are happier than singles, but people with children are the same as childless couples.

★ Republicans are happier than Democrats.

★ People who go to church are happier than those who don't.

★ People with college degrees are happier than those without, but people with advanced degrees are less happy.

- People with an active sex life are happier than those without.

- Women and men are equally happy, but women have a wider emotional range.

- Having an affair will make you happy, but not if your spouse finds out and leaves you.

- People are least happy when they are commuting to work.

- Busy people are happier than those with too little to do.

- Wealthy people are happier than poor ones, but just by a little bit.

- Iceland and Denmark are some of the happiest places.

- Seventy percent of the variability in happiness can be attributed to relationships with people.

Interestingly, among all the variables, the best predictor of happiness is whether people have trust (for example, trust in their country and trust in their government).

Takeaways

- People make quick decisions about what is not trustworthy. So they reject a Web site first, and then decide after that whether or not to actually trust it.

- Design factors, such as color, font, layout, and navigation, are critical in making it through the first "trust rejection" phase.

- If a Web site makes it through the first rejection cut, then content and credibility become the determining factors as to whether the person trusts the site.

80 LISTENING TO MUSIC RELEASES DOPAMINE IN THE BRAIN

Have you ever listened to a piece of music and experienced intense pleasure, even chills? Valorie Salimpoor (2011) and her team conducted research that shows that listening to music can release the neurotransmitter dopamine. Even anticipating music can release dopamine.

The researchers used Positron Emission Tomography scans, fMRI, and psychophysiological measures such as heart rate to measure reactions while people listened to music. The participants provided music that they said gave them intense pleasure and chills. The range of music included classical, folk, jazz, electronica, rock, pop, tango, and more.

PLEASURE VERSUS ANTICIPATED PLEASURE

Salimpoor's team saw the same pattern of brain and body activity when people were listening to their music that they saw when people feel euphoria and craving while getting a reward. The experience of pleasure corresponded with dopamine release in one part of the brain (the striatal dopaminergic system). When people were anticipating a pleasurable part of the music, there was a dopamine release in a different part of the brain (the nucleus accumbens).

Takeaways

* Music can be intensely pleasurable.

* People have favorite music that induces euphoria.

* Music is very individualized. What induces euphoria in one person may have no effect for someone else.

* Anticipating the pleasurable parts of music activates different areas of the brain and neurotransmitters than actually listening to and experiencing the music.

* Allowing people to use or add their own music to whatever Web site, product, design, or activity they're engaging in is a powerful way to engage them in a positive and potentially addictive experience.

81 THE MORE DIFFICULT SOMETHING IS TO ACHIEVE, THE MORE PEOPLE LIKE IT

You've heard about fraternities that have difficult initiation rituals to get in. The idea is that if an organization is hard to get into, then the people in it like it even more than if entry was not so difficult.

The first research on this initiation effect was done by Elliot Aronson at Stanford University in 1959. Aronson set up three initiation scenarios (severe, medium, and mild, although the severe was not really that severe) and randomly assigned people to the conditions. He did indeed find that the more difficult the initiation, the more people liked the group.

COGNITIVE DISSONANCE THEORY

Leon Festinger (1956) was the social psychologist who developed the idea of *cognitive dissonance theory.* Aronson uses this theory to explain why people like groups that they had to endure hardship to join. People go through this painful experience only to find themselves part of a group that is not all that exciting or interesting. But that sets up a conflict (dissonance) in their thought process—if it's boring and uninteresting, why did I submit myself to pain and hardship? To reduce the dissonance then, you decide that the group is really important and worthwhile. Then it makes sense that you were willing to go through the pain.

SCARCITY AND EXCLUSIVITY

In addition to the theory of cognitive dissonance to explain this phenomenon, I think scarcity comes into play. If it's difficult to join the group, then not very many people can do it. If I might not be able to make it in, then I would lose out. So if I went through a lot of pain, it must be good.

Takeaways

* I'm not suggesting that you make your Web site, product, or software application hard to use so that people will feel pain and therefore like it more, although that is probably accurate.

* If you want people to join your online community, you might find that people use it more and value it more if there are steps that have to be taken to join. Filling out an application, meeting certain criteria, being invited by others—all of these can be seen as barriers to entry, but they may also mean that the people who do join care more about the group.

82 PEOPLE OVERESTIMATE REACTIONS TO FUTURE EVENTS

Here's a thought experiment. On a scale of 1 to 10, with 1 being the lowest and 10 being the highest, rate how happy you are right now. Write that number down. Now imagine that you win the lottery today. You now have more money than you ever thought you would. You have millions and millions of dollars. What do you think your happiness rating would be at the end of today? Write that number down. What do you think your happiness rating will be two years from now, if you win millions and millions in the lottery today?

PEOPLE ARE POOR PREDICTORS

In his book, *Stumbling on Happiness* (2007), Daniel Gilbert discusses the research he and others have conducted on predicting or estimating emotional reactions to events. He has found that people greatly overestimate their own reactions to both pleasant and unpleasant events in their lives. Whether it's predicting how they'll respond to a negative event (such as losing a job, having an accident, or the death of a loved one) or a positive one (such as coming into a lot of money, landing a dream job, or finding the perfect mate), everyone tends to overestimate their reaction. If the event is negative, they predict that they'll be very upset and devastated for a long time. If the event is positive, they predict that they'll be deliriously happy for a long time.

A BUILT-IN REGULATOR

What really happens is that you have a built-in regulator. Whether negative events happen, or positive events happen, you stay at about the same level of happiness most of the time. Some people are generally happier or less happy than others, and this level of happiness stays constant no matter what happens to them. This means that people are not very accurate in their predictions of future happiness.

Takeaways

✳ Be careful of believing customers who tell you that making a particular change to a product or a design will make them much happier with it, or cause them to never use it again.

✳ People may prefer one thing over another or think that they will, but their reaction, be it positive or negative, will probably not be as strong as they imagine it.

83 PEOPLE FEEL MORE POSITIVE BEFORE AND AFTER AN EVENT THAN DURING IT

Imagine you're planning a trip with your sister to the Cayman Islands several months from now. The two of you talk on the phone at least once a week, discuss the snorkeling you plan to do, and talk about restaurants that are close to the place you are staying. You look forward to the trip for a long time.

Contrast that with the actual experience of the trip and you may find that the anticipation was better than the trip. In fact, Terence Mitchell (1997) and his team conducted research on just such a situation. They studied people who were taking a trip to Europe, a short trip over the Thanksgiving holiday weekend, or a three-week bicycle tour of California.

Before the event people looked forward to the trip with positive emotions, but during the trip their ratings of the trip were not that positive. The little disappointments that always occur while traveling colored their emotional landscape to the point where they felt less positive about the trip in general. Interestingly, a few days after the trip, the memories became rosy again.

 How to have a great vacation and great memories

While we're on the subject of vacations, here's some interesting information from a variety of research that can help you get the most enjoyment out of your vacation:

★ Several short vacations are better than one long one.

★ The end of the vacation affects your long-term memory more than the beginning or the middle.

★ Having an intense, peak experience makes you more likely to remember the trip positively, even if the intense experience wasn't necessarily positive.

★ Interrupting a trip makes you enjoy the uninterrupted part even more.

Takeaways

✳ If you're designing an interface where people are planning something in the future (winning the lottery, going on a trip, arranging a business event, building a house), they'll have more positive feelings about the experience the longer you can draw out the planning phase.

✳ If you measure satisfaction or other feelings, realize that you'll get more positive ratings if you ask people a few days after the interaction, than if you ask them while they're interacting with the product or Web site.

84 PEOPLE WANT WHAT IS FAMILIAR WHEN THEY'RE SAD OR SCARED

It's Friday afternoon and your boss calls you in to say that he's not happy with your latest project report. This is the project that you repeatedly told him was in trouble and you asked that more staff be assigned. You feel all your warnings were ignored. Now he's telling you that this work will reflect badly on you and you may even lose your job. On the way home you stop at the grocery store. You are sad and scared. Will you buy the cereal you always buy, or will you try something new?

PEOPLE WANT WHAT'S FAMILIAR

According to research by Marieke De Vries (2010) of Radboud University Nijmegen, in the Netherlands, you will buy the familiar brand. Research shows that people want what is familiar when they are sad or scared. They are willing to try something new and different when they're in a happy mood and not as sensitive to what is familiar.

THE DESIRE FOR THE FAMILIAR IS RELATED TO THE FEAR OF LOSS

This craving for the familiar and a preference for familiar brands is probably tied to the basic fear of loss. In my book *Neuro Web Design: What Makes Them Click?* I talk about the fear of loss. When people are sad or scared, the old brain and the mid-brain (emotional) are on alert. They have to protect themselves. And a quick way to be safe is to go with what you know. A strong brand is familiar. A strong logo is familiar. So when people are sad or scared, they'll go for a brand and logo they know.

 It's easy to change someone's mood

It turns out that it is remarkably easy to affect people's moods, especially in the short term (for instance, long enough for them to make a purchase at a Web site). In Marieke De Vries's research, participants watched video clips of the Muppets (to instigate a good mood) versus clips from the movie *Schindler's List* (to instigate a bad mood). People reported their mood as significantly elevated after the Muppets and significantly lowered after *Schindler's List*. This mood change then affected their actions in the rest of the research study.

Takeaways

✳ Brands are a shortcut. If someone has had a positive experience with a brand in the past, then that brand is a signal of safety to the old brain.

✳ Brands are just as important, or even more important, online. In the absence of being able to see and touch the actual product, the brand becomes the surrogate for the experience. This means that brands have a lot of power when people are making an online purchase.

✳ Messages of fear or loss may be more persuasive if your brand is an established one.

✳ Messages of fun and happiness may be more persuasive if your brand is a new one.

PEOPLE MAKE
MISTAKES

To err is human, to forgive divine.
—ALEXANDER POPE

People make mistakes. It's impossible to build a system that is impervious to human error. This chapter is all about the errors that people make.

85 PEOPLE WILL ALWAYS MAKE MISTAKES; THERE IS NO FAIL-SAFE PRODUCT

I collect computer error messages. It's kind of a hobby. Some of them date back to the old character-based computer screens. Most of them weren't trying to be humorous; they were written by computer programmers who were trying to explain what was going wrong. But many of them end up being quite funny, and some of them intentionally so. My favorite was from a company in Texas. When there was a "fatal" error, meaning the system was going to crash, a message came up that said, "Shut 'er down Henry, she's spewin' up mud!"

ASSUME THAT SOMETHING WILL GO WRONG

The reality is that something always goes wrong: a user makes a mistake in working with a computer, or a company releases software that has too many errors, or a designer develops something that is unusable because he or she doesn't understand what the user needs to do. Everyone makes mistakes.

It is very difficult to create a system that is free of all errors, and that guarantees that people won't make mistakes. In fact it's impossible. Ask the people at Three Mile Island, or Chernobyl, or British Petroleum. The more costly the errors are, the more you need to avoid them. The more you need to avoid them, the more expensive it is to design the system. If it's critical that people not make mistakes (for example, if you're designing a nuclear power plant, or an oil rig, or a medical device), then be prepared. You'll have to test two or three times more than usual, and you'll have to train two or three times longer. It's expensive to design a fail-safe system. And you will never fully succeed.

THE BEST ERROR MESSAGE IS NO ERROR MESSAGE

Error messages are probably the part of a device or software program that gets the least amount of time and energy, and maybe that is appropriate. After all, *the best error message is no error message* (meaning that the system is designed so that no one makes errors). But when something goes wrong, it's important that people know what to do about it.

How to write an error message

Assuming that an error will occur and that you'll need to inform the person using your design, make sure that your error message does the following:

- ★ Tells the person what he or she did

- ★ Explains the problem

- ★ Instructs the person how to correct it

- ★ Is written in plain language using active, not passive, voice

- ★ Shows an example

Here is an example of a poor error message:

> #402: Before the invoice can be paid it is necessary that the invoice payment be later than the invoice create date.

Say instead, "You entered an invoice payment date that is earlier than the invoice create date. Check the dates and reenter so that the invoice payment date is after the invoice create date."

Takeaways

＊ Think ahead to what the likely mistakes will be. Figure out as much as you can about the kinds of mistakes people are going to make when they use what you've designed. And then change your design before it goes out so that those mistakes won't be made.

＊ Create a prototype of your design and get people to use it so you can see what the errors are likely to be. When you do this, make sure the people who are testing the prototype are the same people who will be using it. For example, if the product is designed for nurses in a hospital, don't use your designers down the hall to test for errors. You need to have nurses at a hospital test for errors.

＊ Write error messages in plain language and follow the guidelines above for clear error messages.

---

86 PEOPLE MAKE ERRORS WHEN THEY ARE UNDER STRESS

On a trip not too long ago I found myself in a hotel room outside Chicago with my 19-year old daughter moaning in pain. She'd been sick for a week, each day with a new symptom, but that morning everything got worse—her eardrum felt like it was going to burst. Should I cancel my client meeting and take her to an urgent care clinic? Because I was traveling, I was "out of network," so I first had to call my insurance provider to find out if there were "in network" doctors we could go to and still be covered by our plan. The customer service representative told me to go to a particular Web site, and said that any doctor we picked through that site would be considered "in network."

USING A WEB SITE UNDER STRESS

With my daughter still moaning in the background, I went to the URL I was given on the phone. The first field on the first page had me stumped. The form asked for the type of plan I had (**Figure 86.1**).

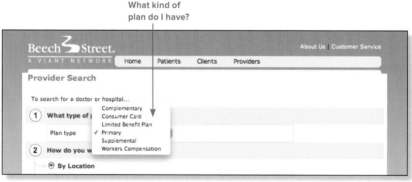

FIGURE 86.1 The first field on the form

Unsure, I left it at the default (Primary) and moved on to the next field. My daughter was still wailing. Next I had to decide how I wanted to search. I filled in the form and pressed the Search button. The screen came back saying I'd made errors. I went through this several times. It was time for me to leave for my meeting. What should I do? The more stressed I got, the more trouble I had filling in the form. I gave up, and gave my daughter some ibuprofen and a warm cloth for her ear. I turned on the TV, handed her the remote, and went to my client meeting. I took her to a clinic later that day when I could think clearly.

Several days later I brought the page up again on my computer screen. Looking at it a few days later, I decided there were some design and usability issues, but overall, it wasn't that confusing. When I was very stressed, however, the Web page was daunting and impossible to use, and not at all intuitive.

THE YERKES-DODSON LAW

Research on stress shows that a little stress (called *arousal* in the field of psychology) can help you perform a task, because it heightens awareness. Too much stress, however, degrades performance. Two psychologists, Robert Yerkes and John Dodson, (1908) first postulated this arousal/performance relationship, and hence it has been called the Yerkes-Dodson law for over a century (**Figure 86.2**).

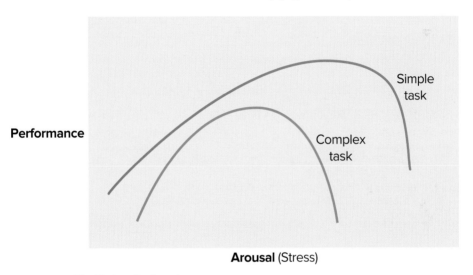

FIGURE 86.2 The Yerkes-Dodson law

Arousal helps up to a point

The Yerkes-Dodson law states that performance increases with physiological or mental arousal, but only up to a point. When levels of arousal become too high, performance decreases. Research shows that the optimal amount of stress/arousal depends on the difficulty of the task. Difficult tasks require less arousal to reach optimal performance, and will start to break down if the arousal level is too high. Simpler tasks require more arousal and don't fall off as fast.

Tunnel action sets in

When arousal first goes up there is an energizing effect, as the person is paying attention. But as the stress increases there are negative effects. Attention gets unfocused, people have trouble remembering, problem solving degrades, and tunnel action sets in. Tunnel action is where you keep doing the same task over and over, even though it isn't working.

Physical evidence of the Yerkes-Dodson law

Sonia Lupien and her team (2007) looked at the relationship of glucocorticoids—hormones related to stress—and memory performance. The researchers found the same upside down U curve as the Yerkes-Dodson law when tracking the amount of glucocorticoids in the bloodstream.

TASKS ARE MORE STRESSFUL THAN YOU MAY THINK

Don't assume that people will use your product in a stress-free environment. Things that may not seem stressful to you as a designer might be very stressful for the person using your product in the real world. Assembling a toy at midnight on the night before a child's birthday party is stressful. Trying to fill out a form on a screen when a customer is present on the phone or in person is stressful. Most medical situations are stressful. One of my clients had people filling out a form for approving whether medical procedures would be covered by insurance. "It's just a form," was what my client said. But when we interviewed the people using the screens they said they were very worried they would make a mistake on the form. "What if I make a mistake and someone doesn't get a procedure paid for as a result?" one of them asked. They felt a huge responsibility. It was a stressful situation.

Men and women may react differently to stress

Lindsay St. Claire (2010) and her team found that if men drank caffeinated coffee while completing a stressful task, it impaired their performance. Women, on the other hand, completed the task faster if they had been drinking caffeinated coffee.

Sweets and sex reduce stress

Yvonne Ulrich-Lai (2010) and her team fed sugar drinks to rats and measured their physiological and behavioral reactions to stress. The sugar drink calmed down the amygdala and reduced stress hormones and cardiovascular effects of stress. Sexual activity did the same.

 ## When the stakes go up, errors may appear

Alex Rodriguez of the New York Yankees was set to hit his 600th career home run in the summer of 2010. He hit number 599 on July 22, but then spent almost two weeks trying to get one more to make it 600. And this was not the first time he took a long time getting to the number he wanted. Back in 2007 he had the same problem getting from 499 to 500.

This is an example of making mistakes when the stakes are high—a typical problem when dealing with well-learned skills and behaviors. When a skill is practiced and well-learned, it's done primarily in an unconscious way. When the stakes go up you tend to overanalyze. Overanalyzing a well-learned skill works for novices, but causes errors for experts.

Takeaways

* If people are performing a boring task, then you need to raise the level of arousal with sound, colors, or movement.

* If people are doing a difficult task, then you need to lower the level of arousal by eliminating any distracting elements such as color, sounds, or movement, unless they are directly related to the task at hand.

* If people are under stress, they won't see things on the screen, and they'll tend to do the same actions over and over, even if they don't work.

* Do research to find out which situations might be stressful. Make site visits, observe and interview the people who are using your product, determine the level of stress, and then redesign if stress is present.

* If someone is an expert at a well-learned task, then performance stress may cause errors.

87 NOT ALL MISTAKES ARE BAD

Dimitri van der Linden (2001) and his team conducted research on exploration strategies that people employ when learning how to use computers and electronic devices. Van der Linden's idea is that errors have consequences, but, contrary to popular belief, not all consequences are negative. Although it's possible, and even likely, that making an error has a negative consequence, it's also likely that the error has a positive or a neutral outcome.

Errors with a positive consequence are actions that do not give the desired result, but provide the person with information that helps him or her achieve an overall goal.

Errors with a negative consequence are those that result in a dead end, undo a positive consequence, send the person back to a starting point, or result in action that cannot be reversed.

Errors with a neutral consequence are errors that have no effect on task completion.

For example, let's say that you've designed a new tablet to compete with the iPad. You give people an early prototype to see how usable the device is. They move the slider bar that they think is the volume control, but instead the screen gets brighter. They've chosen the brightness slider, rather than the volume slider. It's a mistake, but now they know how to make the screen brighter. If that's a feature that they also need to learn to accomplish the task of watching a video (and assuming they do eventually find the volume slider), then we could say that the error had a positive consequence.

Now let's say that they're trying to move a file from one folder to another, but they misunderstand the meaning of the button choices and they delete the file instead. That's an error that has negative consequences.

Finally, they try to select a menu option that is not available. They've made an error, but the consequence is neither positive nor negative—it's neutral.

Takeaways

* Although you don't want people to make lots of errors when using your product, errors will occur.

* Since you know there will be errors, look for and document them during user testing. Note whether each error consequence is positive, negative, or neutral.

* After user testing (and even before it), concentrate on redesigning to minimize or avoid errors with negative consequences first.

88 PEOPLE MAKE PREDICTABLE TYPES OF ERRORS

In addition to thinking about the consequences of errors, as in the van der Linden study described previously, there is another useful error taxonomy. The Morrell (2000) taxonomy classifies two types of errors: performance and motor-control.

PERFORMANCE ERRORS

Performance errors are mistakes you make while you're going through the steps to complete a procedure. Morrell further divides performance errors into commission errors, omission errors, or wrong-action errors.

Commission errors

Let's say you're trying to get a task done, such as turning on the Wi-Fi on your tablet. All you have to do is touch the On/Off control on the screen, but you think that you also need to touch the drop-down menu and select the network. That's an example of a commission error: you took additional steps that were unnecessary.

Omission errors

Now let's say that you're setting up e-mail on your new tablet. You enter your e-mail address and password. What you don't realize is that you have to set up your outgoing and incoming mail settings; you've only set up the outgoing ones. In this case you omitted steps; this is called an omission error.

Wrong-action errors

Let's go back to setting up email. You enter your email and address, but you enter the wrong server name for your email outgoing server. That is an example of a wrong-action error. You took an action at the appropriate point in the procedure, but it was the wrong action.

MOTOR-CONTROL ERRORS

Motor-control errors are those you make while using the controls of a device. Let's say you're trying to get used to using your fingers to rotate a picture on your tablet. But instead of rotating the picture, you go to the next picture. In this case you've made a motor-control error.

You may have different errors that you want to track as you design or conduct user testing. The important thing is to decide ahead of time which types of errors you think people will make, and which are important for you to detect and correct.

 The Swiss cheese model of human error

In his book *Human Error* (1990), James Reason wrote that errors have a cumulative effect. **Figure 88.1** starts with an error in the organization, which then leads to additional errors in supervision, which leads to even more errors. Each error makes a hole in the system until the end when you have Swiss cheese (lots of holes), eventually leading to a human error that is a mishap. Reason used nuclear power plant disasters as his example.

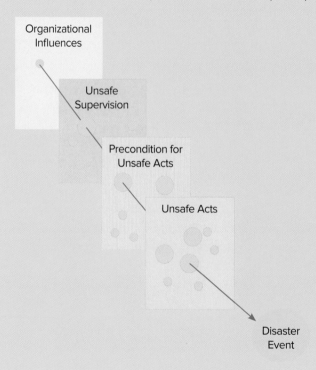

FIGURE 88.1 James Reason's Swiss cheese model of human error

In 2000 Scott Shappell and Douglas Wiegmann wrote a paper on HFACS for the U.S. Office of Aviation Medicine. They worked from James Reason's Swiss cheese model and extended it to propose a system for analyzing and classifying human errors. They focused on preventing errors in aviation, such as pilot error and control tower error. **Figure 88.2** shows an example of the types of errors an HFACS can classify and analyze.

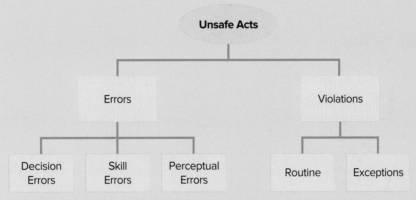

FIGURE 88.2 Types of errors an HFACS classifies

Takeaways

* People will make different types of errors in learning about and using your product. Before you conduct user testing or user observation, decide on the possible errors you are most concerned about.

* During user testing and observation, collect data on which category of errors people are making. This will help focus your redesign efforts after testing.

* If you're in a field where errors are not just annoying or inefficient, but actually may result in accidents or loss of human lives, then you should use a system like HFACS to analyze and prevent errors.

89 PEOPLE USE DIFFERENT ERROR STRATEGIES

In addition to classifying the types of errors that people make, you can think about the types of strategies that people use to correct an error. Neung Eun Kang and Wan Chul Yoon (2008) conducted a research study to look at the types of errors that both younger and older adults make when learning how to use new technologies. In their study they identified and tracked different error strategies.

SYSTEMATIC EXPLORATIONS

When people use systematic exploration, this means that they plan out what procedures they'll use to correct the error. For example, let's say that they're trying to figure out how to put a song on a repeat loop on their tablet. They try one menu and that doesn't work, so they set out to see what each item in the menu system does for the music part of the device. They start at the first item in the first menu and works their way through all the choices in the part of the tablet controls related to playing music. They are exploring systematically.

TRIAL AND ERROR EXPLORATIONS

In contrast to systematic exploration, trial and error means that the person randomly tries out different actions, menus, icons, and controls.

RIGID EXPLORATIONS

Doing the same action over and over, even though it doesn't solve the error, is called rigid exploration. For example, let's say someone wants a song to repeat in a loop on their tablet and touches an icon on the screen that they think should set the song to loop. But it doesn't work. They then choose the song again, and press the icon again. And they keep repeating this combination of actions, even though it doesn't work.

Older adults complete tasks differently than younger adults

Kang and Yoon (2008) found no difference in completion rates for tasks due to age, but older adults (those in their forties and fifties) used different strategies than younger adults (those in their twenties).

★ Older adults took more steps to get the tasks completed, mainly because they made more errors as they went along, and they tended to use more rigid exploration strategies than younger adults.

★ Older adults often failed to receive meaningful hints from their actions and therefore made less progress toward the task goal.

★ Older adults showed more motor-control problems.

★ Older adults didn't use their past knowledge as much as younger adults.

★ Older adults had a higher level of uncertainty about whether their actions were correct. They felt more time pressure and less satisfaction.

★ Older adults adopted more trial and error strategies than younger adults, but analysis of the data showed this was not due to age, but due to lack of background and experience with the type of device.

Takeaways

✳ People use different types of strategies in correcting errors. During user testing and observation, collect data on which strategies your particular audience uses. This information will be helpful in predicting future issues and in redesign.

✳ Don't assume that a population will be unable to finish a task just because they're older. They may do it differently, and it may take more time, but they may be able to complete as many tasks as younger people.

✳ In addition to thinking about younger versus older people, think about novices versus experts. All older people are not the same. Just because someone is 60 years old doesn't mean they lack experience with computers. It's possible for a 60-year-old to be a computer geek who has used computers for a long time and has lots of knowledge. It's also possible for a 20-year-old to have less experience with a particular product, device, or software.

HOW PEOPLE
DECIDE

The way people decide to take an action is less straightforward than we think. In this chapter we look at the science of how people make decisions.

90 PEOPLE MAKE MOST DECISIONS UNCONSCIOUSLY

You're thinking of buying a TV. You do some research on what TV to buy and then go online to purchase one. What factors are involved in this decision-making process? It may not be the process you think it is. In my book *Neuro Web Design: What Makes Them Click?* I explain that people like to think that they've carefully and logically weighed all the relevant factors before they make a decision. In the case of the TV, you've considered the size of TV that works best in your room, the brand that you've read is the most reliable, the competitive price, whether this is the best time to buy, and so on. You've considered all those factors consciously, but research on decision making shows that your actual decision is made primarily in an unconscious way.

Unconscious decision making includes factors such as

★ What other people are deciding to buy: "I see that a particular TV got high ratings and reviews at the Web site."

★ What is consistent with your persona (commitment): "I'm the kind of person who always has the latest thing, the newest technology."

★ Whether you can pay off any obligations or social debts with this purchase (reciprocity): "My brother has had me over to his house all year to watch the games. I think it's time we had them over to our place to watch, so I'd better get a TV at least as good as his."

★ Fear of loss: "This TV is on sale, and if I don't buy it right now the price may go up and I might not be able to buy one for a long time."

★ Your particular drives, motivations, and fears.

UNCONSCIOUS DOESN'T MEAN IRRATIONAL OR BAD

Most of our mental processing is unconscious, and most of our decision making is unconscious, but that doesn't mean it's faulty, irrational, or bad. We're faced with an overwhelming amount of data (millions of pieces of data come into the brain every second!) and our conscious minds can't process all of it. The unconscious has evolved to process most of the data and to make decisions for us according to guidelines and rules of thumb that are in our best interest most of the time. This is the genesis of "trusting your gut," and most of the time it works.

Takeaways

✳ To design a product or Web site that persuades people to take a certain action, you need to know the unconscious motivations of your target audience.

✳ When people tell you their reasons for deciding to take a certain action, you have to be skeptical about what they say. Because decision making is unconscious, they may be unaware of the true reasons for their decisions.

✳ Even though people make decisions based on unconscious factors, they want a rational, logical reason for the decisions they make. So you still need to provide the rational, logical reasons, even though they're unlikely to be the actual reasons that people decided to take action.

91 THE UNCONSCIOUS KNOWS FIRST

One of my favorite pieces of research on unconscious mental processing was conducted by Antoine Bechara (1997) and his team. Participants in the study played a gambling game with decks of cards. Each person received $2,000 of pretend money. They were told that the goal was to lose as little of the $2,000 as possible, and to try to make as much over the $2,000 as possible. There were four decks of cards on the table. Each participant turned over a card from any of the four decks, one card at a time, and continued turning over cards from the deck of their choice until the experimenter told them to stop. The subjects didn't know when the game would end. They were told that they earned money every time they turned over a card. They were also told that sometimes when they turned over a card, they earned money but also *lost* money (by paying it to the experimenter). The participants didn't know any of the rules of the gambling game. Here are what the rules actually were:

★ If they turned over any card in decks A or B, they earned $100. If they turned over any card in decks C and D, they earned $50.

★ Some cards in decks A and B also required participants to pay the experimenter a lot of money, sometimes as much as $1,250. Some cards in decks C and D also required participants to pay the experimenter, but the amount they had to pay was only an average of $100.

★ Over the course of the game, decks A and B produced net losses if participants continued using them. Continued use of decks C and D rewarded participants with net gains.

The rules never changed. Although participants didn't know this, the game ended after 100 cards had been turned over.

THE UNCONSCIOUS MIND PICKS UP THE DANGER FIRST

Most participants started by trying all four decks. At first, they gravitated toward decks A and B because those decks paid out $100 per turn. But after about 30 turns, most turned to decks C and D. They then continued turning cards in decks C and D until the game ended. During the study, the experimenter stopped the game several times to ask participants about the decks. The participants were connected to a skin conductance sensor to measure their skin conductance response (SCR). The participants' SCR readings were elevated when they played decks A and B (the "dangerous" decks) long before they consciously realized that A and B were dangerous. Their SCRs increased before they touched—or even thought about—using decks A and B. The unconscious knew that decks A and B were "dangerous" and resulted in a loss. This was evidenced by the spike in the SCR. However, that's all unconscious. Their conscious minds didn't yet know that anything was wrong.

Eventually participants said they had a hunch that decks C and D were better, but the SCR shows that the old brain figured this out long before the new brain realized it. By the end of the game, most participants had more than a hunch and could articulate the difference in the two decks, but a full 30 percent of the participants couldn't explain why they preferred decks C and D. They said they just thought those decks were better.

Takeaways

✳ People respond and react to unconscious signals of danger.

✳ The unconscious acts more quickly than the conscious mind. This means that people often take actions or have preferences, but cannot explain why they prefer what they do.

PEOPLE WANT MORE CHOICES AND INFORMATION THAN THEY CAN PROCESS

If you stand in any aisle in any retail store in the U.S., you'll be inundated with choices. Whether you're buying candy, cereal, TVs, or jeans, you'll likely have a huge number of items to choose from. Whether it's a retail store or a Web site, if you ask people if they'd prefer to choose from a few alternatives or have lots of choices, most people will say they want lots of choices.

TOO MANY CHOICES PARALYZES THE THOUGHT PROCESS

Sheena Iyengar's book *The Art of Choosing* (2010) details her research and others' on choice. In graduate school Iyengar conducted what is now known as the "jam" study. Iyengar and Mark Lepper (2000) decided to test the theory that people who have too many choices will not choose at all. They set up booths at a busy upscale grocery store and posed as store employees. They alternated the selection on the table. Half of the time there were six choices of fruit jam for people to try and the other half of the time there were twenty-four jars of jam.

Which table had more visitors?

When there were twenty-four jars of jam, 60 percent of the people coming by would stop and taste. When there were six jars of jam only 40 percent of the people would stop and taste. So having more choices was better, right? Not really.

Which table resulted in more tasting?

You might think that people would taste more jam when the table had twenty-four varieties. But they didn't. People stopped at the table, but they only tasted a few varieties whether there were six or twenty-four choices available. People can remember only three or four things at a time (see the chapter "How People Remember"); likewise they can decide from among only three or four things at a time.

Which table resulted in more purchases?

The most interesting part of Iyengar's study is that 31 percent of the people who stopped at the table with six jars actually made a purchase. But only 3 percent of the people who stopped at the table with twenty-four jars actually made a purchase. So even though more people stopped by, less people purchased. To give you an example of the numbers, if 100 people came by (they actually had more than that in the study, but 100 makes the calculations easy for our purposes), 60 of them would stop and try the jam at the twenty-four-jar table, but only two would make a purchase. Forty people would stop and try the jam at the six-jar table, and twelve of them would actually make a purchase.

WHY PEOPLE CAN'T STOP

So if "less is more," then why do people always want more choices? It's part of that dopamine effect. Information is addictive. It's only when people are confident in their decisions that they stop seeking more information.

Takeaways

* Resist the impulse to provide your customers with a large number of choices.

* If you ask people how many options they want, they will almost always say "a lot" or "give me all the options." So if you ask, be prepared to deviate from what they ask for.

* If possible, limit the number of choices to three or four. If you have to offer more options, try to do so in a progressive way. For example, have people choose first from three or four options, and then choose again from a subset.

93 PEOPLE THINK CHOICE EQUALS CONTROL

In *The Art of Choosing* (2010), Sheena Iyengar describes an experiment with rats. The rats were given a choice of a direct path to food, or a path that had branches and therefore required choices to be made. Both paths resulted in access to the same food in the same amounts. If all the rats wanted was food, then they should take the short, direct path. But the rats continuously preferred the path with branches.

In experiments with monkeys and pigeons, the animals learn to press buttons to get food. If given a choice between one button and multiple buttons, both monkeys and pigeons prefer multiple buttons.

In similar research with humans, people were given chips to use at a casino. They could use the chips at a table that had one roulette wheel, or at a table where they could choose from two roulette wheels. People preferred the table with two wheels, even though all three wheels were identical.

Even though it isn't necessarily true, people equate having choices with having control. If people are to feel in control, then they need to feel that their actions are powerful and that they have choices to make. Sometimes having many choices makes it harder to get what they want, but they still want the choices so that they feel in control of the decision.

The desire to control the environment is built into us. This makes sense, since by controlling the environment we likely increase our chances of surviving.

 The need to control starts young

Iyengar describes a study of infants as young as four months old where the researchers attached the babies' hands to a string. The infants could move their hands to pull the string, which would cause music to play. Then the researchers would detach the string from the music control. They would play music at the same intervals, but the infant had no control over when the music would play. The babies would become sad and angry, even though the music was still playing at the same intervals. They wanted to control when the music played.

Takeaways

✳ People need to feel that they're in control and that they have choices.

✳ People won't always choose the fastest way to complete a task. When you're deciding how your audience will accomplish a task with your Web site or product, you may want to offer more than one way, even if the alternative methods are less efficient, just so that people will have a choice.

✳ Once you've given people choices, they'll be unhappy if you take those choices away. If a new version of your product includes improved methods for accomplishing tasks, you may want to leave some of the older methods in the product so that people feel they have options.

PEOPLE MAY CARE ABOUT TIME MORE THAN THEY CARE ABOUT MONEY

Say you're out for a Sunday bike ride on your favorite path, and you come across some kids selling lemonade. Do you stop and buy lemonade? Do you like the lemonade? Does your buying or liking the lemonade have anything to do with the wording on the sign next to the lemonade stand? Apparently so.

Cassie Mogilner and Jennifer Aaker (2009) from the Stanford Graduate School of Business conducted a series of experiments to see whether references to time or references to money would affect whether people stopped to buy, how much they were willing to pay, and how satisfied they were with the products they bought. They conducted five experiments.

SPENDING TIME VERSUS SPENDING MONEY

The first study was the lemonade stand previously described. Sometimes there was a sign that said, "Spend a little time, and enjoy C & D's lemonade." This was the "time" condition. Sometimes the sign said, "Spend a little money, and enjoy C & D's lemonade" (money condition) and other times the sign said, "Enjoy C & D's lemonade" (control condition).

A total of 391 people passed by either on foot or on bikes. Those who stopped to purchase lemonade ranged in age from 14 to 50, and there was a mix of gender and occupations. Customers could pay anywhere between $1 and $3 for a cup of lemonade—the customer decided on the price. The authors comment that the high price was justified by the fact that the customers got to keep the high-quality plastic cup. After customers drank their lemonade, they completed a survey.

More people stopped to buy lemonade when the sign mentioned time (14 percent). In fact, twice as many people stopped when time was mentioned than when money was mentioned (7 percent). In addition, customers in the time condition paid more money for the lemonade ($2.50 on average) compared to the money condition ($1.38 on average). Interestingly, the control condition was in between on both the number of people stopping to purchase and the average price. In other words, mentioning time brought the most customers and the most money, mentioning money brought the fewest customers and the least money, and mentioning neither was in between. The same was true when customers filled out the satisfaction survey.

The researchers came up with the hypothesis that when you invoke time in the message, you make more of a personal connection than when you invoke money. To test this idea, they conducted four more experiments in the lab rather than in the field to see how the time versus money messaging affected people's ideas about purchasing iPods, laptops, jeans, and cars.

PEOPLE WANT TO CONNECT

At the end of all the experiments, the researchers concluded that people are more willing to buy, spend more money, and like their purchases better if there's a personal connection. In most cases, that personal connection is triggered by references to time instead of money. The idea is that mentioning time highlights your experience with the product, and this thinking about the experience makes the personal connection.

However, for certain products (such as designer jeans or prestige cars) or for certain consumers (those who value possessions more than experiences), personal connection is highlighted by mentioning money more than by mentioning time. These people are in the minority, but they are out there.

Takeaways

* The best thing to do, of course, is to know your market or audience. If they're influenced by prestige and possessions, then by all means mention money.

* Be aware that most people, most of the time, are more influenced by time and experiences that produce a personal connection than money or possessions.

* If you don't have the time or budget to know your audience well, and if you're selling nonprestige items or services, then err on the side of time and experiences, and delay the mention of money as long as possible.

95 MOOD INFLUENCES THE DECISION-MAKING PROCESS

You have just been offered a new job. The work is interesting, and there's more money, but there are downsides, too. You'll probably have to travel more and work longer hours. Should you take the new job or stay where you are? Your gut tells you to go for it, but when you sit down and make a list of pros and cons, the cons outweigh the pros, and the logical method tells you to stay put. Which will you follow: your gut or your logic?

Marieke de Vries (2008) and her team conducted research to find out. They were interested in the intersection between mood and decision-making strategies.

Participants were shown a video clip of a funny part from a Muppets movie (happy mood), or the movie *Schindler's List* (sad mood). Next they were shown some Thermos products. Some participants were told to choose which Thermos they'd like to win in a lottery based on their first feeling (intuitive condition). Other participants were instructed to evaluate the different products in terms of the pros and cons of their features and attributes (deliberative condition).

After the participants chose the Thermos they preferred, they estimated the monetary value of their Thermos. Next they filled out a questionnaire that measured their current mood, and lastly filled out a questionnaire that rated their usual style of decision making, intuitive or deliberative.

Here is a summary of their results:

★ The video clips worked in terms of getting people into a happy or sad mood.

★ Participants who usually make intuitive decisions estimated the value of the Thermos higher when given intuitive instructions.

★ Participants who usually make deliberate decisions estimated the value of the Thermos higher when given deliberate instructions.

★ Participants in a happy mood estimated the value of the Thermos higher when making an intuitive decision, regardless of their usual decision-making style.

★ Participants in a sad mood estimated the value of the Thermos higher when making a deliberative decision, regardless of their usual decision-making style.

★ There were no gender differences.

Takeaways

∗ Some people tend to make decisions intuitively, and others tend to make them in a deliberate way.

∗ People will estimate a product to be of higher value if they can make the decision in their "natural" style.

∗ If you can find out someone's style, you can suggest to them how to make a decision and that will result in a higher estimation of the value of a product.

∗ You can influence someone's mood easily, for example, with a short video clip.

∗ People in a good mood will rate a product as being more valuable if they are asked to make the decision quickly based on their first feelings.

∗ People in a sad mood will rate a product as being more valuable if they are asked to make the decision in a more deliberate way.

∗ If you influence people's mood, then you can suggest to them how to think about their decision-making process. This will result in a higher estimation of the value of a product or service.

96 GROUP DECISION MAKING CAN BE FAULTY

Walk into any office building in the world and you'll find the conference rooms filled with groups of people meeting and making decisions. Every day, thousands of decisions in businesses and organizations are made by groups large and small. Unfortunately, research shows that group decision making has some serious flaws.

THE DANGER OF GROUP-THINK

Andreas Mojzisch and Stefan Schulz-Hardt (2010) presented people with information on prospective job candidates. Everyone received and reviewed the information on their own first, not together in a face-to-face group. One set of participants received information on the preferences of the other people in the group before they began the review of the material, and another set of participants did not receive information on the preferences of the group before their review. Everyone then received the same information on the candidates. To make the best decision, participants would have had to review all the information given to them.

The researchers found that people who received information on the group's preferences before reviewing the candidate information did not review the candidate information fully, and therefore did not make the best decisions. In a memory test, they did not remember the most relevant information. The researchers concluded that when a group of people starts a discussion by sharing their initial preferences, they spend less time and less attention on the information available outside the group's preferences. And they therefore make a less than optimal decision.

Mojzisch and Schulz-Hardt did a follow-up study where they changed the situation so that the group was together face-to-face. In this study, each group member had different information about the potential job candidates. They could only reach the best decision if all the group members shared their unique information. Again, if the group started by talking about their initial preferences, they paid less attention to the relevant information during the discussion and made the wrong decision.

 Ninety percent of group discussions start off on the wrong foot

Ninety percent of group discussions start with group members talking about their initial impressions. The research is clear that this is a poor idea; instead, by starting the discussion with relevant information, this data will be weighed more carefully for a better decision.

BUT TWO PEOPLE CAN BE BETTER THAN ONE

The wide receiver catches the football right at the corner of the end zone. Is it a touchdown or not? Two referees saw the play from two different angles. Are they more likely to make a correct decision if they talk about it or if they decide individually? Research by Bahador Bahrami shows that "two heads are better than one" if they talk together and if they are both competent in their knowledge and skills.

Bahrami (2010) and his team found that pairs do better than individuals at making decisions as long as they freely discuss their disagreements, not only about what they saw, but also about how confident they are about what they saw. If they aren't allowed to freely discuss, and they just give their decision, then the pair does not make better decisions than an individual would.

Takeaways

＊ If one person is less competent than the others, and that person doesn't realize that he or she is, though the rest of the team does realize it, then the team tends to make poor decisions because they should ignore the less competent member's opinions, but they don't.

＊ Give people a way and time to consider all relevant information on their own before they see what other people think.

＊ Ask people to rate how confident they are in their decision before they show that decision to others.

＊ Once opinion sharing starts, make sure people have enough time to discuss their disagreements.

＊ It's easy for people to share information now, and for that information to be widely disseminated. This free flow of information and opinions may mean that people are collectively making poorer decisions.

97 PEOPLE ARE SWAYED BY A DOMINANT PERSONALITY

Anyone who has made a decision in a group, or facilitated a focus group, has had the experience of seeing and hearing a dominant member of the group monopolize the conversation and the decision. Just because decisions are made in a group setting doesn't mean that the entire group really made the decision. Many people give up in the presence of one or more dominant group members, and may not speak up at all.

WHY DOES THE LEADER BECOME THE LEADER?

Cameron Anderson and Gavin Kilduff (2009) researched group decision making. They formed groups of four students each and had them solve math problems from the GMAT (a standardized test for admission to graduate business school programs). Using standardized math problems allowed the researchers to evaluate how well the group solved the problems they were given. It also allowed them to compare each member's competence by looking at their previous SAT math scores from their undergraduate admission to college.

During the problem-solving session, the researchers videotaped the group conversations and reviewed them later to decide who was the leader of each group. They had multiple sets of observers view the videos to see if there was consensus about who the leaders were. They also asked the people in the groups to identify the leader of their group. Everyone agreed on who the leader was in each group.

Anderson and Kilduff were interested in why the leaders became the leaders. Before the groups started, everyone filled out a questionnaire to measure their level of dominance. As you might imagine, the leaders all scored high on the dominance measure. But that still doesn't suggest how they became leaders. Did they have the best math SAT scores? (No). Did they bully everyone else into letting them be the leader? (No).

The answer surprised the researchers: The leaders spoke first. For 94 percent of the problems, the group's final answer was the first answer that was proposed, and the people with the dominant personalities always spoke first.

Takeaways

✳ If you design as a group, be careful of following the first solution just because it's first.

✳ If you have group meetings (for example, group sessions to make design decisions, or group audience feedback sessions), have each member of the group write down ideas ahead of time and circulate those ideas before the meeting.

98 WHEN PEOPLE ARE UNCERTAIN, THEY LET OTHERS DECIDE WHAT TO DO

Imagine you're browsing a Web site to decide what boots to buy. You see a pair that looks good, but you've never heard of the brand before. Will you buy the boots or not? If you're unsure, then chances are you'll scroll down the page and look for reviews and ratings left by others. And chances are you'll listen to the reviews, even though the people writing the reviews are total strangers.

UNCERTAINTY TIPS THE SCALE

In my book *Neuro Web Design: What Makes Them Click?* I talk about the tendency to look to others to decide what to do. It's called *social validation*.

Bibb Latane and John Darley (1970) conducted research in which they set up ambiguous situations to see if people were affected by what others around them were or were not doing. Participants in the research would go into a room, supposedly to fill out a survey on creativity. In the room would be one or more other people, pretending they were also participants, but who were really part of the experiment. Sometimes there would be one other person in the room, sometimes more. While people were filling out their creativity survey, smoke would start to come into the room from an air vent. Would the participant leave the room? Go tell someone about the smoke? Just ignore it?

PEOPLE TAKE ACTION ONLY IF OTHERS TAKE ACTION

What action, if any, the participant took depended on the behavior of the other people in the room, as well as how many other people there were. The more people, and the more the others ignored the smoke, the more the participant was likely to do nothing. If the participant was alone, he or she would leave the room and notify someone. But if there were others in the room and they didn't react, then the participant would do nothing.

TESTIMONIALS AND RATINGS ARE POWERFUL

Online, social validation is most in evidence with ratings and reviews. When we're unsure about what to do or buy, we look to testimonials, ratings, and reviews to tell us how to behave.

Reviews by others "like me" are the most influential

Yi-Fen Chen (2008) researched three kinds of ratings and reviews at a bookstore Web site: reviews by regular visitors to a Web site, experts on the topic, and recommendations from the Web site itself. All three types influenced behavior, but the reviews by regular visitors were the most influential.

Takeaways

✳ People are very influenced by others' opinions and behaviors, especially when they are uncertain.

✳ Use testimonials, ratings, and reviews if you want to influence behavior.

✳ The more information you provide in the rating and review about the person who left it, the more influential the rating or review will be.

99   PEOPLE THINK OTHERS ARE MORE EASILY INFLUENCED THAN THEY ARE THEMSELVES

I do a lot of writing and speaking on the topic of persuasion. I often talk about John Bargh's research (1996), which shows how much we're influenced by factors that we're not aware of. Bargh had people unscramble sets of words to make sentences. For example, he would ask people to choose four out of five words and make a sentence out of them:

"he florida today lives in"

would become:

"He lives in Florida."

Some people got sets of words that had a theme of "old," such as Florida, retired, old, and elderly. Other people got sets of words that had a young theme, such as youth, energy, and lively. A third group got neutral words that were neither old nor young. After unscrambling the words and making sentences, Bargh would then have the participants walk down the hall to find him. Bargh measured how long it took each person to walk down the hall. People who had been using the "old" words took much longer to walk down the hall. They had been unconsciously affected by the words. But when asked if they thought the words had influenced them, they said no.

When I talk about this research, people believe that others would walk slowly, but that they wouldn't be affected by words in this way.

"I'M NOT THAT INFLUENCED"

In another example, when I discuss the research on *social validation*, such as that regarding ratings and reviews in the previous topic, everyone in the room nods and talks about how it's true that other people are very influenced by ratings and reviews. However, most people I speak to think that they themselves are not very affected. I talk about how much we're affected by pictures, images, and words, and that we don't real- ize we're being influenced. And the reaction is always similar: "Yes, other people are affected by these things, but I'm not."

THE THIRD-PERSON EFFECT

In fact, this belief that "others are affected but not me" is so common that there is research on it, and it has its own name: the *third-person effect*. The research shows that most people think others are influenced by persuasive messages, but that they themselves are not. The research shows that this perception is false. The third-person effect seems to be especially true if you think you aren't interested in the topic. For example, if you're not in the market to buy a new TV, then you'll tend to think that advertising about new TVs won't affect you, but the research says that it will.

WHY DO PEOPLE DECEIVE THEMSELVES THIS WAY?

Why the self-deception? It's partly because all this influence is happening unconsciously. People are literally unaware that they're being influenced. And it's also partly because people don't like to think of themselves as easily swayed, or gullible. To be gullible is to not be in control, and the old brain—the part that is concerned with survival—always wants us to be in control.

Takeaways

* Everyone is affected by unconscious processes.

* If you're doing customer research and people say, "Ratings and reviews don't influence my decision," don't believe what they're saying. Remember that these are unconscious processes, and people are largely unaware of what is affecting them.

100 PEOPLE VALUE A PRODUCT MORE HIGHLY WHEN IT'S PHYSICALLY IN FRONT OF THEM

You go online to reorder a box of your favorite pens. Will you value the product more if the product page has a picture of the pens versus just a text description? Will you think the pens are worth more if you're in the office supply store and the pens were right in front of you? Does it matter if you're buying pens or food or any other product? Does the way the item is displayed at the time you're making the decision affect the dollar value that you put on it? Ben Bushong (2010) and a team of researchers decided to test this out.

In the first set of experiments, the researchers used snack food (potato chips, candy bars, and so on). Participants were given money to spend. There were lots of choices, and the participants could pick what they wanted to buy. (They screened out people on a diet, and people with eating disorders.) Participants "bid" on the products so the researchers could find out what the participants were willing to pay for each product.

Some participants only read the name and a brief description of the item, for example, "Lay's Potato Chips in a 1.5 oz bag." Some saw a picture of the item. And some had the real item right in front of them.

Figure 100.1 shows the results.

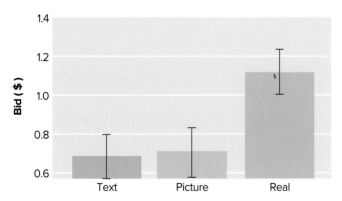

FIGURE 100.1 People valued the food more when it was in front of them

THE REAL DEAL COUNTS

Having a picture didn't increase the amount of money people were willing to bid for the product, but having the product right in front of them definitely did, by up to 60 percent. Interestingly, the form of presentation didn't change how much people said they *liked* the item, just the dollar value they were willing to bid. In fact, some items that they said before the experiment they didn't like, they still valued more highly if they were in front of them.

TOYS, TRINKETS, AND PLEXIGLAS

Next the researchers tried the experiment with toys and trinkets instead of food. **Figure 100.2** shows the results with toys and trinkets. The chart looks the same as with the snack foods.

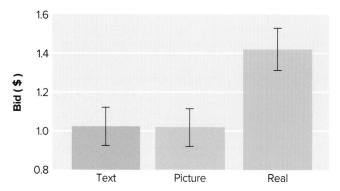

FIGURE 100.2 People valued the toys and trinkets more when they were physically present

WHAT ABOUT SAMPLES?

Deciding to try another tack, the researchers went back to food items, but this time they let people see and taste a sample. The actual item wasn't there, but the sample was. Surely, they thought, the sample would be the same as having the actual item in front of them. Wrong again! **Figure 100.3** shows that the samples were still not as powerful as having the full product available.

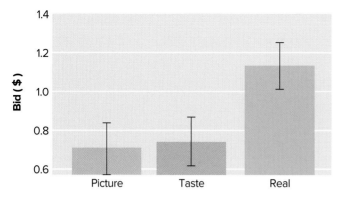

FIGURE 100.3 Samples (taste) were less effective than the actual product

The researchers note that in this taste condition, the participants didn't even look at the samples in the paper cup, since they knew they were the same as the food in the package.

IS IT OLFACTORY?

The researchers wondered if the food produced some unconscious olfactory (smell) cues that triggered the brain, so they did another experiment, putting the food in view, but behind Plexiglas. If the food was in view, but behind Plexiglas, it was deemed to be worth a little more money, but not the same as if it were within reach. "Ah!" the researchers thought, "There are olfactory cues!" but then they found the same result with the nonfood items, so smell is not the trigger. **Figure 100.4** shows the results for the Plexiglas trials.

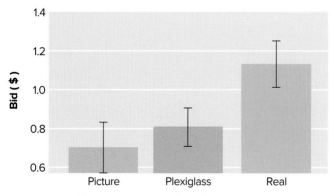

FIGURE 100.4 Plexiglas improved the value, but still not as much as having the product in close physical proximity

A PAVLOVIAN RESPONSE?

Bushong and his team hypothesize that there's a Pavlovian response going on: when the product is actually available, it acts as a conditioned stimulus and elicits a response. Images and even text could potentially become a conditioned stimulus and produce the same response, but they have not been set up in the brain to trigger the same response as the actual item.

Takeaways

* Brick-and-mortar stores may retain an edge if they have products on hand, especially when it comes to price.

* Having a product behind glass or any other kind of barrier may lower the price that the customer is willing to pay.

REFERENCES

Alloway, Tracy P., and Alloway, R. 2010. "Investigating the predictive roles of working memory and IQ in academic attainment." *Journal of Experimental Child Psychology* 80(2): 606–21.

Anderson, Cameron, and Kilduff, G. 2009. "Why do dominant personalities attain influence in face-to-face groups?" *Journal of Personality and Social Psychology* 96(2): 491–503.

Anderson, Richard C., and Pichert, J. 1978. "Recall of previously unrecallable information following a shift in perspective." *Journal of Verbal Learning and Verbal Behavior* 17: 1–12.

Aronson, Elliot, and Mills, J. 1959. "The effect of severity of initiation on liking for a group." *U.S. Army Leadership Human Research Unit*.

Baddeley, Alan D. 1994. "The magical number seven: Still magic after all these years?" *Psychological Review* 101: 353–6.

Baddeley, Alan D. 1986. *Working Memory*. New York: Oxford University Press.

Bahrami, Bahador, Olsen, K., Latham, P. E., Roepstorff, A., Rees, G., and Frith, C. D. 2010. "Optimally interacting minds." *Science* 329(5995): 1081–5. doi:10.1126/science.1185718.

Bandura, Albert. 1999. "Moral disengagement in the perpetration of inhumanities." *Personality and Social Psychology Review* 3(3): 193–209. doi:10.1207/s15327957pspr0303_3, PMID 15661671.

Bargh, John, Chen, M., and Burrows, L. 1996. "Automaticity of social behavior: Direct effects of trait construct and stereotype." *Journal of Personality and Social Psychology* 71(2): 230–44.

Bayle, Dimitri J., Henaff, M., and Krolak-Salmon, P. 2009. "Unconsciously perceived fear in peripheral vision alerts the limbic system: A MEG study." *PLoS ONE* 4(12): e8207. doi:10.1371/journal.pone.0008207.

Bechara, Antoine, Damasio, H., Tranel, D., and Damasio, A. 1997. "Deciding advantageously before knowing advantageous strategy." *Science* 275: 1293–5.

Begley, Sharon. 2010. "West brain, East brain: What a difference culture makes." *Newsweek*, February 18, 2010.

Bellenkes, Andrew H., Wickens, C. D., and Kramer, A. F. 1997. "Visual scanning and pilot expertise: The role of attentional flexibility and mental model development." *Aviation, Space, and Environmental Medicine* 68(7): 569–79.

Belova, Marina A., Paton, J., Morrison, S., and Salzman, C. 2007. "Expectation modulates neural responses to pleasant and aversive stimuli in primate amygdala." *Neuron* 55: 970–84.

Berman, Marc G., Jonides, J., and Kaplan, S. 2008. "The cognitive benefits of interacting with nature." *Psychological Science* 19: 1207–12.

Berns, Gregory S., McClure, S., Pagnoni, G., and Montague, P. 2001. "Predictability modulates human brain response to reward." *The Journal of Neuroscience* 21(8): 2793–8.

Berridge, Kent, and Robinson, T. 1998. "What is the role of dopamine in reward: Hedonic impact, reward learning, or incentive salience?" *Brain Research Reviews* 28: 309–69.

Biederman, Irving. 1985. "Human image understanding: Recent research and a theory." *Computer Vision, Graphics, and Image Processing.* Elsevier.

Broadbent, Donald. 1975. "The magic number seven after fifteen years." Volume 32, Issue 1, October 1985, Pages 29–73. In *Studies in Long-Term Memory,* edited by A. Kennedy and A. Wilkes. London: Wiley.

Bushong, Ben, King, L. M., Camerer, C. F., and Rangel, A. 2010. "Pavlovian processes in consumer choice: The physical presence of a good increases willingness-to-pay." *American Economic Review* 100: 1–18.

Canessa, Nicola, Motterlini, M., Di Dio, C., Perani, D., Scifo, P., Cappa, S. F., and Rizzolatti, G. 2009. "Understanding others' regret: A FMRI study." *PLoS One* 4(10): e7402.

Carey, Susan. 1986. "Cognitive science and science education." *American Psychologist* 41(10): 1123–30.

Cattell, James M. 1886. "The time taken up by cerebral operations." *Mind* 11: 377–92.

Chabris, Christopher, and Simons, D. 2010. *The Invisible Gorilla.* New York: Crown Archetype.

Chartrand, Tanya L., and Bargh, J. 1999. "The chameleon effect: The perception-behavior link and social interaction." *Journal of Personality and Social Psychology* 76(6): 893–910.

Chen, Yi-Fen. 2008. "Herd behavior in purchasing books online." *Computers in Human Behavior* 24: 1977–92.

Christoff, Kalina, Gordon, A. M., Smallwood, J., Smith, R., and Schooler, J. 2009. "Experience sampling during fMRI reveals default network and executive system contributions to mind wandering." *Proceedings of the National Academy of Sciences* 106(21): 8719–24.

Chua, Hannah F., Boland, J. E., and Nisbett, R. E. 2005. "Cultural variation in eye movements during scene perception." *Proceedings of the National Academy of Sciences* 102: 12629–33.

Clem, Roger, and Huganir, R. 2010. "Calcium-permeable AMPA receptor dynamics mediate fear memory erasure." *Science* 330(6007): 1108–12.

Cowan, Nelson. 2001. "The magical number 4 in short-term memory: A reconsideration of mental storage capacity." *Behavioral and Brain Sciences* 24: 87–185.

Craik, Kenneth. 1943. *The Nature of Explanation.* Cambridge (UK) University Press.

Csikszentmihalyi, Mihaly. 2008. *Flow: The Psychology of Optimal Experience.* New York: Harper and Row.

Custers, Ruud, and Aarts, H. 2010. "The unconscious will: How the pursuit of goals operates outside of conscious awareness." *Science* 329(5987): 47–50. doi:10.1126/science.1188595.

Darley, John, and Batson, C. 1973. "From Jerusalem to Jericho: A study of situational and dispositional variables in helping behavior." *Journal of Personality and Social Psychology* 27: 100–108.

Davis, Joshua I., Senghas, A., Brandt, F., and Ochsner, K. 2010. "The effects of BOTOX injections on emotional experience." *Emotion* 10(3): 433–40.

Deatherage, B. H. 1972. "Auditory and other sensory forms of information presentation." In *Human Engineering Guide to Equipment Design*, edited by H. P. Van Cott and R. G. Kincade. Washington, DC: U.S. Government Printing Office.

De Vries, Marieke, Holland, R., Chenier, T., Starr, M., and Winkielman, P. 2010. "Happiness cools the glow of familiarity: Psychophysiological evidence that mood modulates the familiarity-affect link." *Psychological Science* 21: 321–8.

De Vries, Marieke, Holland, R., and Witteman, C. 2008. "Fitting decisions: Mood and intuitive versus deliberative decision strategies." *Cognition and Emotion* 22(5): 931–43.

Dietrich, Arne. 2004. "The cognitive neuroscience of creativity." *Psychonomic Bulletin and Review* 11(6): 1011–26.

Duchenne, Guillaume. 1855. *De l'Électrisation Localisée et de son Application à la Physiologie, à la Pathologie et à la Thérapeutique.* Paris: J.B. Baillière.

Dunbar, Robin. 1998. *Grooming, Gossip, and the Evolution of Language.* Cambridge, MA: Harvard University Press.

Dyson, Mary C. 2004. "How physical text layout affects reading from screen." *Behavior and Information Technology* 23(6): 377–93.

Ebbinghaus, Hermann. 1886. "A supposed law of memory." *Mind* 11(42).

Emberson, Lauren L., Lupyan, G., Goldstein, M., and Spivey, M. 2010. "Overheard cell-phone conversations: When less speech is more distracting." *Psychological Science* 21(5): 682–91.

Ekman, Paul. 2007. *Emotions Revealed: Recognizing Faces and Feelings to Improve Communication and Emotional Life,* 2nd ed. New York: Owl Books.

Ekman, Paul. 2009. *Telling Lies: Clues to Deceit in the Marketplace, Politics, and Marriage*, 3rd ed. New York: W. W. Norton.

Festinger, Leon, Riecken, H. W., and Schachter, S. 1956. *When Prophecy Fails.* Minneapolis: University of Minnesota Press.

Gal, David, and Rucker, D. 2010. "When in doubt, shout." *Psychological Science.* October 13, 2010.

Garcia, Stephen, and Tor, A. 2009. "The N effect: More competitors, less competition." *Psychological Science* 20(7): 871–77.

Genter, Dedre, and Stevens, A. 1983. *Mental Models.* Lawrence Erlbaum Associates.

Gibson, James. 1979. *The Ecological Approach to Visual Perception.* Boston: Houghton Mifflin.

Gilbert, Daniel. 2007. *Stumbling on Happiness*. New York: A.A. Knopf.

Goodman, Kenneth S. 1996. *On Reading.* Portsmouth, NH: Heinemann.

Haidt, Jonathan, Seder, P., and Kesebir, S. 2008. "Hive psychology, happiness, and public policy." *Journal of Legal Studies* 37.

Hancock, Jeffrey T., Currya, L. E., Goorhaa, S., and Woodworth, M. 2008. "On lying and being lied to: A linguistic analysis of deception in computer-mediated communication." *www.informaworld.com* 45(1): 1–23.

Hancock, Jeffrey T., Thom-Santelli, J., and Ritchie, T. 2004. "Deception and design: the impact of communication technology on lying behavior." *Proceedings of the SIGHCHI Conference on Human Factors in Computing Systems.* New York: ACM.

Havas, David A., Glenberg, A. M., Gutowski, K. A., Lucarelli, M. J., and Davidson, R. J. 2010. "Cosmetic use of botulinum toxin-A affects processing of emotional language." *Psychological Science* 21(7): 895–900.

Hsee, Christopher K., Yang, X., and Wang, L. 2010. "Idleness aversion and the need for justified busyness." *Psychological Science* 21(7): 926–30.

Hubel, David H., and Wiesel, T. N. 1959. "Receptive fields of single neurones in the cat's striate cortex." *Journal of Physiology* 148: 574–91.

Hull, Clark L. 1934. "The rats' speed of locomotion gradient in the approach to food." *Journal of Comparative Psychology* 17(3): 393–422.

Hupka, Ralph, Zbigniew, Z., Jurgen, O., Reidl, L., and Tarabrina, N. 1997. "The colors of anger, envy, fear, and jealousy: A cross-cultural study." *Journal of Cross-Cultural Psychology* 28(2): 156–71.

Hyman, Ira, Boss, S., Wise, B., McKenzie, K., and Caggiano, J. 2009. "Did you see the unicycling clown? Inattentional blindness while walking and talking on a cell phone." *Applied Cognitive Psychology.* doi:10.1002/acp.1638.

Iyengar, Sheena. 2010. *The Art of Choosing.* New York: Twelve.

Iyengar, Sheena, and Lepper, M. R. 2000. "When choice is demotivating: Can one desire too much of a good thing?" *Journal of Personality and Social Psychology* 70(6): 996–1006.

Ji, Daoyun, and Wilson, M. 2007. "Coordinated memory replay in the visual cortex and hippocampus during sleep." *Nature Neuroscience* 10: 100–107.

Johnson-Laird, Philip. 1986. *Mental Models.* Cambridge, MA: Harvard University Press.

Kahn, Peter H., Jr., Severson, R. L., and Ruckert, J. H. 2009. "The human relation with nature and technological nature." *Current Directions in Psychological Science* 18: 37–42.

Kang, Neung E., and Yoon, W. C. 2008. "Age- and experience-related user behavior differences in the use of complicated electronic devices." *International Journal of Human-Computer Studies* 66: 425–37.

Kanwisher, Nancy, McDermott, J., and Chun, M. 1997. "The fusiform face area: A module in human extrastriate cortex specialized for face perception." *Journal of Neuroscience* 17(11): 4302–11.

Kawai, Nobuyuki, and Matsuzawa, T. 2000. "Numerical memory span in a chimpanzee." *Nature* 403: 39–40.

Keller, John M. 1987. "Development and use of the ARCS model of instructional design." *Journal of Instructional Development* 10(3): 2–10.

Kivetz, Ran, Urminsky, O., and Zheng, U. 2006. "The goal-gradient hypothesis resurrected: Purchase acceleration, illusionary goal progress, and customer retention." *Journal of Marketing Research* 39: 39–58.

Knutson, Brian, Adams, C., Fong, G., and Hummer, D. 2001. "Anticipation of increased monetary reward selectively recruits nucleus accumbens." *Journal of Neuroscience* 21.

Koo, Minjung, and Fishbach, A. 2010. "Climbing the goal ladder: How upcoming actions increase level of aspiration." *Journal of Personality and Social Psychology* 99(1): 1–13.

Krienen, Fenna M., Pei-Chi, Tu, and Buckner, Randy L. 2010. "Clan mentality: Evidence that the medial prefrontal cortex responds to close others." *The Journal of Neuroscience* 30(41): 13906–15. doi:10.1523/JNEUROSCI.2180-10.2010.

Krug, Steve. 2005. *Don't Make Me Think!* Berkeley, CA: New Riders.

Krumhuber, Eva G., and Manstead, A. 2009. "Can Duchenne smiles be feigned? New evidence on felt and false smiles." *Emotion* 9(6): 807–20.

Kurtzberg, Terri, Naquin, C. and Belkin, L. 2005. "Electronic performance appraisals: The effects of e-mail communication on peer ratings in actual and simulated environments." *Organizational Behavior and Human Decision Processes* 98(2): 216–26.

Lally, Phillippa, van Jaarsveld, H., Potts, H., and Wardle, J. 2010. "How are habits formed: Modelling habit formation in the real world. "*European Journal of Social Psychology* 40(6): 998–1009.

Larson, Adam, and Loschky, L. 2009. "The contributions of central versus peripheral vision to scene gist recognition." *Journal of Vision* 9(10:6): 1–16. doi:10.1167/9.10.6.

Latane, Bibb, and Darley, J. 1970. *The Unresponsive Bystander.* Upper Saddle River, NJ: Prentice Hall.

LeDoux, Joseph. 2000. "Emotion circuits in the brain." *Annual Review of Neuroscience* 23: 155–84.

Lehrer, Jonah. 2010. "Why social closeness matters." *The Frontal Cortex* blog. http://bit.ly/fkGlgF

Lepper, Mark, Greene, D., and Nisbett, R. 1973. "Undermining children's intrinsic interest with extrinsic rewards." *Journal of Personality and Social Psychology* 28: 129–37.

Loftus, Elizabeth, and Palmer, J. 1974. "Reconstruction of automobile destruction: An example of the interaction between language and memory." *Journal of Verbal Learning and Verbal Behavior* 13: 585–9.

Looser, Christine E., and Wheatley, T. 2010. "The tipping point of animacy: How, when, and where we perceive life in a face." *Psychological Science* 21(12): 1854–62.

Lupien, Sonia J., Maheu, F., Tu, M., Fiocco, A., and Schramek, T. E. 2007. "The effects of stress and stress hormones on human cognition: Implications for the field of brain and cognition." *Brain and Cognition* 65: 209–37.

Mandler, George. 1969. "Input variables and output strategies in free recall of categorized lists." *The American Journal of Psychology* 82(4).

Mason, Malia, F., Norton, M., Van Horn, J., Wegner, D., Grafton, S., and Macrae, C. 2007. "Wandering minds: The default network and stimulus-independent thought." *Science* 315(5810): 393–5.

Medina, John. 2009. *Brain Rules.* Seattle, WA: Pear Press.

Mednick, Sara, and Ehrman, M. 2006. *Take a Nap! Change Your Life.* New York: Workman Publishing Company.

Miller, George A. 1956. "The magical number seven plus or minus two: Some limits on our capacity for processing information." *Psychological Review 63*: 81–97.

Mischel, Walter, Ayduk, O., Berman, M., Casey, B. J., Gotlib, I., Jonides, J., Kross, E., Wilson, N., Zayas, V., and Shoda, Y. 2010. "Willpower over the life span: Decomposing self-regulation." *Social Cognitive and Affective Neuroscience*, in press.

Mitchell, Terence R., Thompson, L., Peterson, E., and Cronk, R. 1997. "Temporal adjustments in the evaluation of events: The 'rosy view.'" *Journal of Experimental Social Psychology* 33(4): 421–48.

Mogilner, Cassie and Aaker, J. 2009. "The time versus money effect: Shifting product attitudes and decisions through personal connection." *Journal of Consumer Research* 36: 277–91.

Mojzisch, Andreas, and Schulz-Hardt, S. 2010. "Knowing others' preferences degrades the quality of group decisions." *Journal of Personality and Social Psychology* 98(5): 794–808.

Mondloch, Catherine J., Lewis, T. L., Budrea, D. R., Maurer, D., Dannemiller, J. L., Stephens, B. R., and Keiner-Gathercole, K. A. 1999. "Face perception during early infancy." *Psychological Science* 10: 419–22.

Morrell, Roger, et al. 2000. "Effects of age and instructions on teaching older adults to use Eldercomm, an electronic bulletin board system." *Educational Gerontology* 26: 221–35.

Naquin, Charles E., Kurtzberg, T. R., and Belkin, L. Y. 2010. "The finer points of lying online: e-mail versus pen and paper." *Journal of Applied Psychology* 95(2): 387–94.

Neisser, Ulric, and Harsh, N. 1992. "Phantom flashbulbs: False recollections of hearing the news about Challenger. " In *Affect and Accuracy in Recall,* edited by E. Winograd and U. Neisser. Cambridge (UK) University Press: 9–31.

Norman, Don. 1988. *The Psychology of Everyday Things.* Published in 2002 as *The Design of Everyday Things.* New York: Basic Books.

Ophir, Eyal, Nass, C., and Wagner, A. 2009. "Cognitive control in media multitaskers." *Proceedings of the National Academy of Sciences,* September 15, 2009. http://www.pnas.org/content/106/37/15583

Paap, Kenneth R., Newsome, S. L., and Noel, R. W. 1984. "Word shape's in poor shape for the race to the lexicon." *Journal of Experimental Psychology: Human Perception and Performance* 10: 413–28.

Palmer, Stephen E., Rosch, E., and Chase, P. 1981. "Canonical perspective and the perception of objects." In *Attention and Performance IX,* edited by J. Long and A. Baddeley. Hillsdale, NJ: Erlbaum.

Perfect, Timothy, Wagstaff, G., Moore, D., Andrews, B., Cleveland, V., Newcombe, K., and Brown, L. 2008. "How can we help witnesses to remember more? It's an (eyes) open and shut case." *Law and Human Behavior* 32(4): 314–24.

Pierce, Karen, Muller, R., Ambrose, J., Allen, G., and Courchesne, E. 2001. "Face processing occurs outside the fusiform 'face area' in autism: Evidence from functional MRI." *Brain* 124(10): 2059–73.

Pink, Daniel. 2009. *Drive.* New York: Riverhead Books.

Provine, Robert. 2001. *Laughter: A Scientific Investigation.* New York: Viking.

Ramachandran, V. S. 2010. TED talk on mirror neurons: http://bit.ly/aaiXba

Rao, Stephen, Mayer, A., and Harrington, D. 2001. "The evolution of brain activation during temporal processing." *Nature and Neuroscience* 4: 317–23.

Rayner, Keith. 1998. "Eye movements in reading and information processing: 20 years of research." *Psychological Review* 124(3): 372–422.

Reason, James. 1990. *Human Error.* New York: Cambridge University Press.

Salimpoor, Valorie, N., Benovoy, M., Larcher, K., Dagher, A., and Zatorre, R. 2011. "Anatomically distinct dopamine release during anticipation and experience of peak emotion to music." *Nature Neuroscience.* doi:10.1038/nn.2726.

Sauter, Disa, Eisner, F., Ekman, P., and Scott, S. K. 2010. "Cross-cultural recognition of basic emotions through nonverbal emotional vocalizations." *Proceedings of the National Academy of Sciences* 107(6): 2408–12.

Shappell, Scott A., and Wiegmann, Douglas, A. 2000. "The Human Factors Analysis and Classification System–HFACS." *U.S. Department of Transportation Federal Aviation Administration, February 2000 Final Report.*

Sillence, Elizabeth, Briggs, P. Fishwick, L., and Harris, P. 2004. "Trust and mistrust of online health sites." *CHI'04 Proceedings of the SIGCHI Conference on Human Factors in Computer Systems.* New York: ACM.

Solso, Robert, Maclin, K., and MacLin, O. 2005. *Cognitive Psychology*, 7th ed. Boston: Allyn and Bacon.

Song, Hyunjin, and Schwarz, N. 2008. "If it's hard to read, it's hard to do: Processing fluency affects effort prediction and motivation." *Psychological Science* 19: 986–8.

St. Claire, Lindsay, Hayward, R., and Rogers, P. 2010. "Interactive effects of caffeine consumption and stressful circumstances on components of stress: Caffeine makes men less, but women more effective as partners under stress." *Journal of Applied Social Psychology* 40(12): 3106–29. doi:10.1111/j.1559.

Stephens, Greg, Silbert, L., and Hasson, U. 2010. "Speaker–listener neural coupling underlies successful communication." *Proceedings of the National Academy of Sciences, July 27, 2010.*

Szameitat, Diana, Kreifelts, B., Alter, K., Szameitat, A., Sterr, A., Grodd, W., and Wildgruber, D. 2010. "It is not always tickling: Distinct cerebral responses during perception of different laughter types." *NeuroImage* 53(4): 1264–71. doi:10.1016/j.neuroimage.2010.06.028

Ulrich, Roger S. 1984. "View through a window may influence recovery from surgery." *Science* 224: 420–1.

Ulrich-Lai, Yvonne M., et al. 2010. "Pleasurable behaviors reduce stress via brain reward pathways." *Proceedings of the National Academy of Sciences of the United States of America, November 2010.*

Van Der Linden, Dimitri, Sonnentag, S., Frese, M. and van Dyck, C. 2001. "Exploration strategies, error consequences, and performance when learning a complex computer task." *Behaviour and Information Technology* 20: 189–98.

Van Veen, Vincent, Krug, M. K., Schooler, J. W., and Carter, C. S. 2009. "Neural activity predicts attitude change in cognitive dissonance." *Nature Neuroscience* 12(11): 1469–74.

Wagner, Ullrich, Gais, S., Haider, H., Verleger, R., and Born, J. 2004. "Sleep inspires insight." *Nature* 427(6972): 304–5.

Weiner, Eric. 2009. *The Geography of Bliss.* New York: Twelve.

Weinschenk, Susan. 2008. *Neuro Web Design: What Makes Them Click?* Berkeley, CA: New Riders.

Wiltermuth, Scott, and Heath, C. 2009. "Synchrony and cooperation." *Psychological Science* 20(1): 1–5.

Wohl, M., Pychyl, T., and Bennett, S. 2010. "I forgive myself, now I can study: How self-forgiveness for procrastinating can reduce future procrastination." *Personality and Individual Differences* 48(7): 803–8.

Yarbus, Alfred L. 1967. *Eye Movements and Vision,* translated by B. Haigh. New York: Plenum.

Yerkes, Robert M., and Dodson, J. D. 1908. "The relation of strength of stimulus to rapidity of habit-formation." *Journal of Comparative Neurology and Psychology* 18: 459–482. http://psychclassics.yorku.ca/Yerkes/Law/

Young, Indi. 2008. *Mental Models.* Rosenfeld Media.

Zagefka, Hanna, Noor, M., Brown, R., de Moura, G., and Hopthrow, T. 2010. "Donating to disaster victims: Responses to natural and humanly caused events." *European Journal of Social Psychology.* doi:10.1002/ejsp.781.

Zihui, Lu, Daneman, M., and Reingold, E. 2008. "Cultural differences in cognitive processing style: Evidence from eye movements during scene processing." *CogSci 2008 Proceedings: 30th Annual Conference of the Cognitive Science Society*: July 23–26, 2008, Washington, DC, USA. http://csjarchive.cogsci.rpi.edu/proceedings/2008/pdfs/p2428.pdf

Zimbardo, Philip, and Boyd, J. 2009. *The Time Paradox: The New Psychology of Time That Will Change Your Life.* New York: Free Press.

INDEX

phonological coding, 55
recency and suffix effects, 54
recognition *versus* recall tasks, 53
    inclusion errors, 53
reconstructed memory, 56–57
short-term, 46–47
visual memory *versus* words, 54
working, 46–47
    four items, 48–50
    versus sensory input, 47
mental models, 72–73
    about frequency, 101
    versus conceptual models, 74–75
Mental Models, 72, 73
"Mental Models and Usability," 72
microexpressions, 164
mid-brain, 108
Miller, George A., 48
mind wandering, 68–69
mirror neurons, 147–148, 167
Mischel, Walter, 131
Mississippi state Web site, 133
mistakes people make. *See* errors people make
Mitchell, Terrence, 182
mixed case or lowercase letters *versus*
    uppercase letters, 30–32
Mogilner, Cassie, 210
Mojzisch, Andreas, 214
Mondloch, Catherine, 10
monetary rewards, 126
Morgan, Jacob, 145
Morrell error taxonomy, 195
motivation
    algorithmic to heuristic work, 126
    anticipation *versus* getting, 122
    autonomy, 142
    defaults, 136
    donations for natural *versus* man-made
        disasters, 138
    dopamine system, 121–122
        140-character messages, 124
        breaking dopamine loops, 124
        monetary rewards, 126
        Pavlovian reflex, 123
    forming habits, 139–140
    fundamental attribution errors, 137–138
    goal-gradient effect, 116–117
    gratification, delaying or not, 131
    laziness
        versus happiest when busy, 173
        inherent, 132–135
    mastery incentive, 129–130

number of competitors factor, 141
operant conditioning, 118–120
opioid system, 121
post-reward resetting phenomenon, 117
progress incentive, 127–129
rewards/reinforcements, 116–117
    contingent, 125
    continuous reinforcement schedules,
        120
    interval reward schedules, 118–120
    intrinsic *versus* extrinsic, 125–126
    monetary, 126
    ratio reward schedules, 118–120
    variable rewards, 118–120
    shortcuts, 136
    social incentive, 126
    unconscious, 125
motor loads, 65–67
Müller-Lyer, Franz, 3
multitasking, 105–107
Muppets, 184, 212
muscle movement and emotions, 166–167

N

N effect, 141
Nass, Clifford, 106
The Nature of Explanation, 72
Neisser, Ulric, 60
Neuro Web Design: What Makes Them Click, 70,
    97, 108, 168, 171, 184, 202, 217
new brain, 108
Newton, Issac, 86, 88
Nisbett, Richard, 93, 125
noises that startle, 110–111
Norman, Don, 15

O

object/pattern recognition, 7–8
    affordances, 15
        hyperlinks, 17–18
        incorrect affordances, 16, 18
        perceived affordances, 15–17
        usage cues, 15–16
    canonical perspective, 12
    objects close together, 21
    objects tilted or slight angle above, 11–12
    selective attention, 96
old brain, 108–109, 142
olfactory paths, 169
omission errors, 195
operant conditioning, 118–120